HOOKED ON READING!

128 Wordsearch and Crossword Puzzles Based on the Newbery and Caldecott Award Winners

Marguerite Lewis

Illustrated by Pamela J. Kudla

 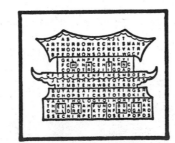 

The Center for Applied Research in Education, Inc.

10 9 8 7

Dedicated to Mike and Emily in
appreciation of their patience
and understanding.

Library of Congress Cataloging-in-Publication Data

Lewis, Marguerite Relyea.
  Hooked on reading.

  Includes bibliographies.
  1. Literary recreations.   2. Word games.   3. Crossword puzzles.   4. Caldecott medal books.   5. Newbery
medal books.   I. Title.
GV1493.L47   1986   793.73   86-2629

ISBN 0-87628-406-3

Printed in the United States of America

ABOUT THE AUTHOR

MARGUERITE LEWIS has been a Library Media Specialist in the Bethlehem Central School District, Delmar, New York since 1969. She received her Bachelor of Science degree from Boston University and her Master's degree in Educational Communications from the State University of New York at Albany.

Mrs. Lewis has published articles, activities, and puzzles in professional and children's magazines. She is the creator of *Library Bingo* and the co-creator, with Pamela J. Lewis Kudla, of *Library Curriculum Flashcards,* both published in 1980 by Larlin Corporation, Marietta, Georgia. Mrs. Lewis is also the author of *Hooked on Research! Ready-to-Use Projects and Crosswords for Practice in Basic Library Skills,* published in 1984 by The Center for Applied Research in Education, Inc.

Mrs. Lewis is a member of the American Library Association and the New York Library Association as well as national, state, and local professional organizations, and has presented many workshops and participated in panel presentations at professional conferences. A book reviewer for *School Library Journal,* Mrs. Lewis is presently assigned as a Library Media Specialist to the Glenmont and Slingerlands elementary schools in the Bethlehem Central School District.

ABOUT THE ILLUSTRATOR

PAMELA J. KUDLA received her Bachelor's degree in Graphic Design from Rochester Institute of Technology, Rochester, New York.

Mrs. Kudla received first prize in the National Paperbox and Packaging Association's 1981 Student Design Competition. She was design consultant for *New York Alive* magazine as well as an assistant art director for Communication and Design, an advertising agency in Latham, New York. The illustrator of *Hooked on Research! Ready-to-Use Projects and Crosswords for Practice in Basic Library Skills,* published in 1984 by The Center for Applied Research in Education, Inc., Mrs. Kudla is currently an art director with B. Sterling Benkhart, Ltd., an advertising and photography studio in Newport, Rhode Island.

ABOUT THIS BOOK

Hooked on Reading! offers 128 ready-to-use wordsearch and crossword puzzles to give elementary and middle school students, grades 3–8, an opportunity to become familiar with the Newbery and Caldecott Awards. Designed for use by both the school librarian and the classroom teacher, this book encourages the students to read and enjoy these award-winning books—and to ask for more!

Section I, "The Newbery Award," presents 72 reproducible wordsearch puzzles that cover each Newbery Award winner from 1922 to 1993. The section begins with a brief introduction to, and history of, the Newbery Award, and a reproducible list of winners each student may use to keep track of the award-winning books he or she has read. In addition, a "Do You Know the Newbery Award Titles?" activity is given so you can test your students' knowledge of the winners. Finally, a "Super Newbery Activities" sheet suggests a variety of addtional projects for your students to do enrichment activities or follow-ups to their reading.

Section II, "The Caldecott Award," offers 56 reproducible crossword puzzles that cover each Caldecott Award winner from 1938 to 1993. This section also begins with a brief introduction to, and history of, the Caldecott Award, along with a reproducible list of award-winning books you can hand out so that each student may keep track of the ones he or she has read.

Complete answer keys for both the Newbery wordsearch puzzles and the Caldecott crossword puzzles are presented in the Answer Key section at the end of the book. A special feature of this book is the annotated bibliographies of the Newbery and Caldecott titles. Found at the back of the book, these bibliographies will help you recommend particular titles to students.

Hooked on Reading! was written to help your students become just that! The puzzles introduce your students to the excellent Newbery and Caldecott award-winning books so that they will appreciate *all* books.

Marguerite Lewis

CONTENTS

SECTION II   THE CALDECOTT AWARD...................... *83*

Caldecott Award Crossword Puzzles:

Contents

THE NEWBERY AWARD
section I

A BRIEF HISTORY OF THE NEWBERY AWARD

In 1921, Frederic Melcher, secretary of the American Booksellers Association, proposed to the American Library Association that an award be established to recognize and honor excellence in children's literature. He further proposed that the award be named in honor of John Newbery, an 18th century English bookseller and publisher of the first books for children.

The proposal was accepted, and the Newbery Award, which was to be given to the author of "the most distinguished contribution to American literature for children published during the preceding year," was established. The early winners were chosen by the members of the American Library Association. Subsequently, a committee was formed to review all published titles and select the winner.

A young sculpter named Rene Chambellan was commissioned to design a medal, which was struck in bronze. Frederic Melcher accepted the financial obligation to have the medal struck each year. His family has continued that tradition to this day.

The winner of the Newbery Award is announced at the midwinter meeting of the American Library Association.

HOW TO USE THIS SECTION

The Newbery Award collection is riding a high crest of popularity today, due to its having been "discovered." For years, librarians eagerly awaited the announcement of the winner, proclaimed its excellence, and then added the newcomer to its dust-collecting colleagues. Every library boasted a complete set of Newbery Award Titles, but the books seldom left the shelves.

Today, many programs, especially for the gifted and talented, have been built around the Newbery collection. This was a natural consequence for several reasons:

- The literature is of excellent quality.
- Combined with the honor books, every genre is represented.
- The collection does not stir up any controversy.
- The collection grows annually.
- The titles are accessible and will stay in print.

The Newbery Award books need to be introduced to students. Students, if left on their own, may gravitate towards less challenging authors; however, when these books are introduced in an interesting and challenging manner, students will read and enjoy them. To help you introduce these books to students this section features:

- "The Newbery Award Winners," a list that can be copied for each student to use as a checklist for choosing a title, locating the book on the shelf, and checking off the title when read.
- "Do You Know the Newbery Award Titles?" an activity that can be completed by an entire class, either working individually or in small groups. This activity can be completed during two instructional class periods or during students' independent time. The answers should be checked together as a class activity.
- "Super Newbery Activities," which challenge those students interested in self-enrichment.
- Seventy-two wordsearch puzzles based on the Newbery Award titles. These puzzles may be used to
        ...familiarize the student with the title
        ...interest the student in reading the book
        ...preview the title
        ...review and reinforce the reading of the book
        ...discuss the story after the book has been read

...prepare the student for an oral book report to the class
...create fun and enjoyment in reading

The Newbery wordsearch puzzles require the students to locate and circle words within a maze. Only those words in the right-hand columns under the puzzles are to be found either forward, backward, horizontally, vertically, diagonally, or a combination of ways. These different combinations of directions in the wordsearch puzzles provide more of a challenge to students because they must often search in more than one direction to find the answer.

THE NEWBERY AWARD WINNERS

Check
Books
Read

1922: Van Loon, *The Story of Mankind*

1923: Lofting, *The Voyages of Doctor Dolittle*

1924: Hawes, *The Dark Frigate*

1925: Finger, *Tales from Silver Lands*

1926: Chrisman, *Shen of the Sea*

1927: James, *Smoky the Cowhorse*

1928: Mukerji, *Gay-Neck, the Story of a Pigeon*

1929: Kelly, *The Trumpeter of Krakow*

1930: Field, *Hitty, Her First Hundred Years*

1931: Coatsworth, *The Cat Who Went to Heaven*

1932: Armer, *Waterless Mountain*

1933: Lewis, *Young Fu of the Upper Yangtze*

1934: Meigs, *Invincible Louisa*

1935: Shannon, *Dobry*

1936: Brink, *Caddie Woodlawn*

1937: Sawyer, *Roller Skates*

THE NEWBERY AWARD WINNERS (continued)

Check
Books
Read

1938: Seredy, *The White Stag*

1939: Enright, *Thimble Summer*

1940: Daugherty, *Daniel Boone*

1941: Sperry, *Call It Courage*

1942: Edmonds, *The Matchlock Gun*

1943: Gray, *Adam of the Road*

1944: Forbes, *Johnny Tremain*

1945: Lawson, *Rabbit Hill*

1946: Lenski, *Strawberry Girl*

1947: Bailey, *Miss Hickory*

1948: du Bois, *The Twenty-One Balloons*

1949: Henry, *King of the Wind*

1950: de Angeli, *The Door in the Wall*

1951: Yates, *Amos Fortune, Free Man*

1952: Estes, *Ginger Pye*

1953: Clark, *Secret of the Andes*

THE NEWBERY AWARD WINNERS (continued)

Check
Books
Read

1954: Krumgold, *And Now Miguel*

1955: DeJong, *The Wheel on the School*

1956: Latham, *Carry On, Mr. Bowditch*

1957: Sorensen, *Miracles on Maple Hill*

1958: Keith, *Rifles for Watie*

1959: Speare, *The Witch of Blackbird Pond*

1960: Krumgold, *Onion John*

1961: O'Dell, *Island of the Blue Dolphins*

1962: Speare, *The Bronze Bow*

1963: L'Engle, *A Wrinkle in Time*

1964: Neville, *It's Like This, Cat*

1965: Wojciechowska, *Shadow of a Bull*

1966: Treviño, *I, Juan de Pareja*

1967: Hunt, *Up a Road Slowly*

1968: Konigsburg, *From the Mixed-Up Files of Mrs. Basil E. Frankweiler*

1969: Alexander, *The High King*

THE NEWBERY AWARD WINNERS (continued)

Check
Books
Read

1970: Armstrong, *Sounder*

1971: Byars, *Summer of the Swans*

1972: O'Brien, *Mrs. Frisby and the Rats of NIMH*

1973: George, *Julie of the Wolves*

1974: Fox, *The Slave Dancer*

1975: Hamilton, *M.C. Higgins the Great*

1976: Cooper, *The Grey King*

1977: Taylor, *Roll of Thunder, Hear My Cry*

1978: Paterson, *Bridge to Terabithia*

1979: Raskin, *The Westing Game*

1980: Blos, *A Gathering of Days: A New England Girl's Journal*

1981: Paterson, *Jacob Have I Loved*

1982: Willard, *A Visit to William Blake's Inn: Poems for Innocent and Experienced Travelers*

1983: Voigt, *Dicey's Song*

1984: Cleary, *Dear Mr. Henshaw*

1985: McKinley, *The Hero and the Crown*

Name _____   Date _____

THE NEWBERY AWARD WINNERS (continued)

**Check
Books
Read**

1986: MacLachlan, *Sarah, Plain and Tall*

1987: Fleischman, *The Whipping Boy* _____

1988: Freedman, *Lincoln: A Photobiography* _____

1989: Fleischman, *Joyful Noise: Poems for Two Voices* _____

1990: Lowry, *Number the Stars* _____

1991: Spinelli, *Maniac Magee* _____

1992: Naylor, *Shiloh* _____

1993: Ryland, *Missing May* _____

1994: _____

1995: _____

Name _____   Date _____

DO YOU KNOW THE NEWBERY AWARD TITLES?

1. Which eight titles contain names of animals?

_____

_____

_____

_____

_____

_____

_____

_____

2. Which two titles contain names of birds?

_____

_____

3. Which two titles contain names of seasons?

_____

_____

4. Which three titles contain names of weapons?

_____

_____

_____

5. Which title contains the name of a vegetable?

_____

6. Which title contains the name of a fruit?_____

7. Which title contains the name of a spice?

_____

Name ______________________ Date ______________________

DO YOU KNOW THE NEWBERY AWARD TITLES? (continued)

8. Which six titles contain girls' names?

____

____

____

____

____

____

9. Which nine titles contain boys' names?

____

____

____

____

____

____

____

____

____

10. Judging from the titles, which six books take place outside the United States?

____

____

____

____

____

____

DO YOU KNOW THE NEWBERY AWARD TITLES? (continued)

11. Which four titles contain the names of colors?

_____

_____

_____

_____

12. Which three titles contain the word "king"?

_____

_____

_____

13. Which two titles contain numbers?

_____

_____

14. Which title is a diary or a journal?

_____

15. Which three titles contain the word "Miss" or "Mrs."?

_____

_____

_____

16. Which was the first title to win the Newbery Award?

_____

17. Which two titles contain the word "Mr."?

_____

_____

18. Which is the shortest title?

_____

Name _____   Date _____

DO YOU KNOW THE NEWBERY AWARD TITLES? (continued)

19. Which is the longest title?

_____

20. Which two titles contain words associated with weather?

_____

_____

21. Which title sounds like a science fiction story?

_____

22. Which six titles contain geographical terms?

_____

_____

_____

_____

_____

_____

23. Which two titles contain words that make you think of something round?

_____

_____

24. Which title contains a word associated with sewing?

_____

25. Which title contains part of a king's costume?

_____

26. Which two titles contain words associated with music?

_____

_____

DO YOU KNOW THE NEWBERY AWARD TITLES? (continued)

27. Which two titles are collections of literature?

_____

_____

28. Which two titles contain words of affection?

_____

_____

29. Which title sounds like a game?

_____

30. Which two titles contain initials?

_____

_____

SUPER NEWBERY ACTIVITIES

Before Reading a Newbery Winner

1. Select a book that sounds interesting based on the title.
2. Complete the wordsearch puzzle for that particular title.
3. Explain in writing what the puzzle tells you about the book and what you feel might happen in the book, based only on the puzzle.
4. Read the book. Compare your beforehand thoughts with the actual story.

After Reading a Newbery Winner

1. Complete the wordsearch puzzle for that particular title.
2. Make a list of the "Words and Topics of Interest" section of the wordsearch puzzle. Explain the significance of each in the story.

After Reading a Newbery Winner

1. Read the Newbery Honor book for a particular year.
2. Compare the Honor book with the Award winner, emphasizing
   a. plot
   b. character development
   c. literary quality
3. If you were a member of the Newbery Committee, which title would you have chosen as the Honor book and the Award winner? Why?

After Reading a Newbery Winner

1. Read the Newbery Honor book for a particular year.
2. Using the format of a wordsearch puzzle, design a wordsearch for the Honor book.
3. Share the wordsearch puzzle with your classmates.

Name _____   Date _____

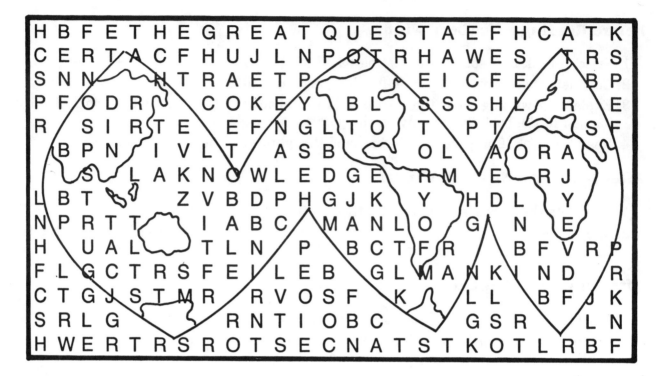

The words in the right-hand column may be found forward, backward, diagonally, horizontally, vertically, or a combination of these.

Words to Find

Author	HENDRIK VAN LOON
Title	THE STORY OF MANKIND
Main Character	MAN
Setting	PLANET EARTH
Words and Topics of Interest	KEY, ANCESTORS, CIVILIZATION, BELIEFS, LIFE, DEATH, STRUGGLE, KNOWLEDGE
Type of Story	HISTORY
Newbery Honor Book	HAWES, THE GREAT QUEST

On the back of this sheet, write why you think *The Story of Mankind* sounds interesting.

Name _____   Date _____

The Voyages of Doctor Dolittle by Hugh Lofting (1923)   *I–2*

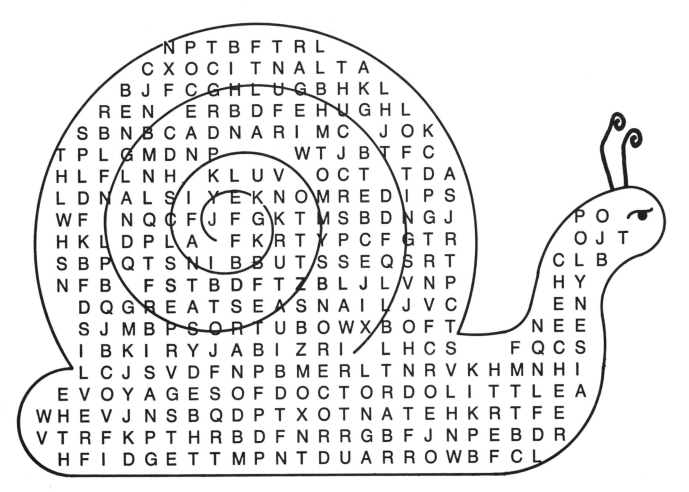

The words in the right-hand column may be found forward, backward, diagonally, horizontally, vertically, or a combination of these.

Words to Find

Author   ....   HUGH LOFTING

Title   ....   <u>THE VOYAGES OF DOCTOR DOLITTLE</u>

Main Character   ....   TOMMY STUBBINS

Supporting Characters   ....   JOHN DOLITTLE, POLYNESIA, JIP, CHEE CHEE, MIRANDA

Setting   ....   ENGLAND, ATLANTIC OCEAN

Words and Topics of Interest   ....   LONG ARROW, SPIDERMONKEY ISLAND, SILVER FIDGET, JABIZRI, GREAT SEA SNAIL

Type of Story   ....   FANTASY

Newbery Honor Book   ....   NO RECORD

On the back of this sheet, write why you think *The Voyages of Doctor Dolittle* sounds interesting.

The Dark Frigate by Charles Boardman Hawes (1924)

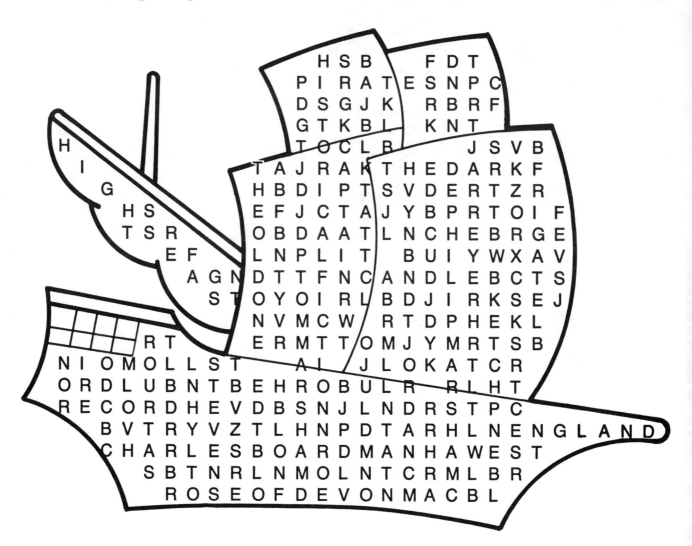

The words in the right-hand column may be found forward, backward, diagonally, horizontally, vertically, or a combination of these.

Words to Find

Author	CHARLES BOARDMAN HAWES
Title	THE DARK FRIGATE
Main Character	PHILIP MARSHAM
Supporting Characters	TOM MARSHAM, MOLL STEVENS, CAPTAIN CANDLE, THE OLD ONE, TOM JORDAN
Setting	ENGLAND, HIGH SEAS
Words and Topics of Interest	PIRATES, KETCH, ROSE OF DEVON
Type of Story	HISTORICAL FICTION
Newbery Honor Book	NO RECORD

On the back of this sheet, write why you think *The Dark Frigate* sounds interesting.

Name _____   Date _____

Tales from Silver Lands by Charles J. Finger (1925)

The words in the right-hand column may be found forward, backward, diagonally, horizontally, vertically, or a combination of these.

```
F S G R T
A T B V A T
N O H M L P Q B T
T R C Y E E B F E
R H Y H S S O U T H A
T O T A B F P E Q J M K N
O L E R C R L V B T E R P A K
A O L L R O E D H D R E A M C J
  G L E Y M S E H S I W R Y O
  Y E S F S T C R B C X R P A
    R J F I N G E R A F I K C
    T S L A M I N A H S T H
    J V W C B D E G H K
      E R M Z B E X
      R U A T R Q B
      L E G E N D S
      A L I R B T
      N D C F N S
      D B V A D
      S O I R
      G I
      B E
        V
        I   T
        L   C
```

Words to Find

Author	CHARLES J. FINGER
Title	<u>TALES FROM SILVER LANDS</u>
Main Character	STORYTELLER
Supporting Characters	PEOPLE, ANIMALS, BIRDS
Setting	SOUTH AMERICA
Words and Topics of Interest	LEGENDS, MAGIC, EVIL, WISHES, GIANTS
Type of Story	ANTHOLOGY
Newbery Honor Book	PARRISH, <u>DREAM COACH</u>

On the back of this sheet, write why you think *Tales from Silver Lands* sounds interesting.

Shen of the Sea by Arthur Bowie Chrisman (1926) **I—5**

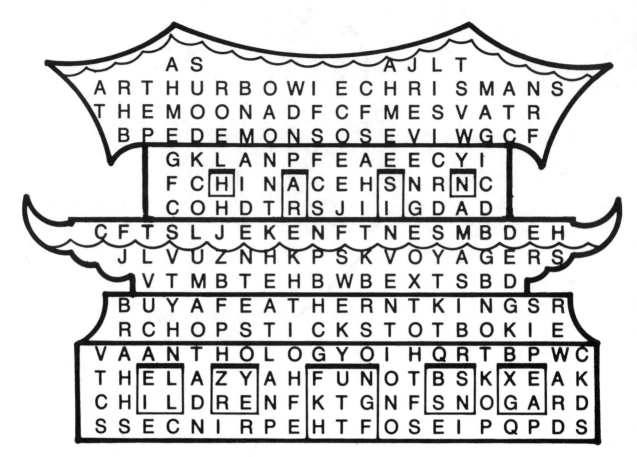

The words in the right-hand column may be found forward, backward, diagonally, horizontally, vertically, or a combination of these.

Words to Find

Author	ARTHUR BOWIE CHRISMAN
Title	SHEN OF THE SEA
Sampling	BUY A FEATHER, AH-MEE'S INVENTION, THE LAZY AH-FUN, PIES OF THE PRINCESS, MANY WIVES, THE MOON MAIDEN, CHOP STICKS
Setting	CHINA
Words and Topics of Interest	CHILDREN, DEMONS, DRAGONS, MAGIC, REWARD, REVENGE
Type of Story	ANTHOLOGY
Newbery Honor Book	COLUM, VOYAGERS

On the back of this sheet, write why you think *Shen of the Sea* sounds interesting.

Name _____   Date _____

The words in the right-hand column may be found forward, backward, diagonally, horizontally, vertically, or a combination of these.

Words to Find

Author .... WILL JAMES

Title .... SMOKY THE COWHORSE

Main Character .... SMOKY

Supporting Characters .... MAMMY, CLINT

Setting .... AMERICAN WEST

Words and Topics of Interest .... BRANDING, WOLVES, BLIZZARD, COWBOYS, HOME RANCH, ROUND UP, ROCKING R, THE COUGAR, CLOUDY

Type of Story .... ANIMAL FICTION

Newbery Honor Book .... NO RECORD

On the back of this sheet, write why you think *Smoky the Cowhorse* sounds interesting.

Gay-Neck, the Story of a Pigeon by Dhan Gopal Mukerji (1928)   **I—7**

The words in the right-hand column may be found forward, backward, diagonally, horizontally, vertically, or a combination of these.

Words to Find

Author	DHAN GOPAL MUKERJI
Title	GAY-NECK, THE STORY OF A PIGEON
Main Character	GAY-NECK
Supporting Characters	DHAN, GHOND, RADJA, HIRI
Setting	INDIA
Words and Topics of Interest	BROODED, EAGLES, BAZ, WORLD WAR, MESSAGES, PEACE
Type of Story	FANTASY
Newbery Honor Book	SNEDEKER, DOWNRIGHT DENCEY

On the back of this sheet, write why you think *Gay-Neck, the Story of a Pigeon* sounds interesting.

Name _____   Date _____

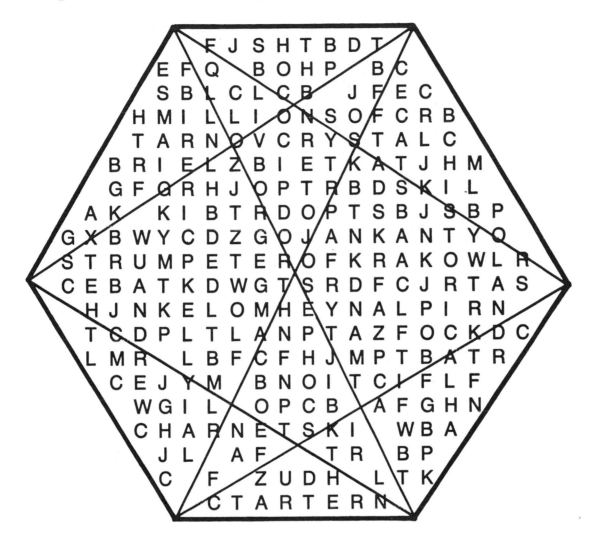

The words in the right-hand column may be found forward, backward, diagonally, horizontally, vertically, or a combination of these.

Words to Find

Author	ERIC P. KELLY
Title	THE TRUMPETER OF KRAKOW
Main Character	JOSEPH
Supporting Characters	ANDREW CHARNETSKI, ELZBIETKA, JAN KANTY
Setting	POLAND
Words and Topics of Interest	TARNOV CRYSTAL, TARTER, PAN, HEYNAL, WOLF
Type of Story	HISTORICAL FICTION
Newbery Honor Book	GAG, MILLIONS OF CATS

On the back of this sheet, write why you think *The Trumpeter of Krakow* sounds interesting.

Name _____   Date _____

Hitty, Her First Hundred Years by Rachel Field (1930)

The words in the right-hand column may be found forward, backward, horizontally, vertically, or a combination of these.

```
        P
      C B       F H
      H I T T Y H G D
      J         N L E O A
    T S         B L R R U
    D F         E A F A G
  K S Q         S I C H H
  A T L K N C   L T S R T
  L I T T L E   M H T E E
  N E V B T X W E H L R R
  P T S B H L   D U I F O
  H J A L U E   E N T E F
  S F E H I Q N   C R D L H T
  H N X M P B U K L L R D E Q S
  R I T P L H K A F Z A B E P S L N
  S B P H O E B E K U R R C D I E F Y U
  C F H G S I V Y E L T I R Y H I T T Y
  S D E T I N U N R E T S A E B N F O T
  T F B A T C T U B C S V A C E H R
  A D E G I S A B E L L A C R A F
  T E A T O N J H L N     S
  E H F A N T A S Y F
  S M A I N E D A E
  M O U N T A I N
  T U D D
  C R O W
    B
    E
    N
```

Words to Find

Author	RACHEL FIELD
Title	HITTY, HER FIRST HUNDRED YEARS
Main Character	HITTY
Supporting Characters	PHOEBE, LITTLE THANKFUL, CLARISSA
Setting	EASTERN UNITED STATES
Words and Topics of Interest	MOUNTAIN ASH, CROW, SHIP, QUAKER, EXPOSITION, MAINE
Type of Story	FANTASY
Newbery Honor Book	EATON, DAUGHTER OF THE SEINE

On the back of this sheet, write why you think *Hitty, Her First Hundred Years* sounds interesting.

The Cat Who Went to Heaven by Elizabeth Coatsworth (1931) **I–10**

The words in the right-hand column may be found forward, backward, diagonally, horizontally, vertically, or a combination of these.

```
    T  J  L
  R  C  F  G  K
     N  B  F
     Z  C  R  B
  T  H  E  C  A  T  W  H  O  W  E  N  T  T  O
  B  W  T  L  P  H  S  I  R  R  A  P  D  H  J
  E  L  I  Z  A  B  E  T  H  C  Q  T  R  E  B  A
  F  K  J  A  O  L  N  R  P  O  G  J  H  A  L  P  A
  H  B  T  Z  Q  R  E  B  A  C  V  B  V            N
  G  O  O  D     H  L  J  T  M  T  C  E
     L  F  B  O  I  R  S  R     J  N
     S     K  O  U  Q  G  T  W  Q     P  L  H
  T  N     M  R  D  E  I  V  O  R  S  D  T     B
  A  R  T  I  S  T  D  G  O  O  R     H  I  J     K
  L  D  C     U  H  R  U  T  T  J  R  N        R
  N  Y  S  A  T  N  A  F  S  K  H  B  O        K  N
  W  D  C  B  E  F  H  J  M  P  L  N  R  S  V  P
  F  L  O  A  T  I  N  G  I  S  L  A  N  D
  H  O  U  S  E  K  E  E  P  E  R  I
```

Words to Find

Author	ELIZABETH COATSWORTH
Title	THE CAT WHO WENT TO HEAVEN
Main Character	ARTIST
Supporting Characters	HOUSEKEEPER, GOOD FORTUNE
Setting	JAPAN
Words and Topics of Interest	BUDDHA
Type of Story	RELIGIOUS FANTASY
Newbery Honor Book	PARRISH, FLOATING ISLAND

On the back of this sheet, write why you think *The Cat Who Went to Heaven* sounds interesting.

Name _____   Date _____

```
S P R A B F T C D F G N H J X Y P M A
U O T W L A U R A A D A M S A R M E R
N J R X K T R L X P R V T U G J F T I
B L I A B H Q C A L I C O B U S H L Z
E T B R H E U F G C B H J N N P H E O
A S A H J R O K L O P A T R S R N A
R E L P I J L S X V Z H A
E L F T S U V E W B C A F G K
R D I L M J E A B G M O T H E R Q P T
X E C N C K W S D E O L N O C D S E H
Y R T L O R R N Z U V S J L K
O B I M M P D X Y P J I L
U R O N A O B O P R S T X O N
N O N I A T N U O M S S E L R E T A W
G T X Z E F H A B C F E I J H M N K
E H U N C L E L Z X D R T U B G H O J
R E Y B C D G R E T S I S T I D R S S
B R O T H E R T S T R U C B F I E L D
```

The words in the right-hand column may be found forward, backward, diagonally, horizontally, vertically, or a combination of these.

Words to Find

Author	LAURA ADAMS ARMER
Title	WATERLESS MOUNTAIN
Main Character	YOUNGER BROTHER
Supporting Characters	MOTHER, FATHER, ELDER BROTHER, UNCLE, SISTER, BIGMAN
Setting	ARIZONA
Words and Topics of Interest	SUN BEARER, TURQUOISE WOMAN, LEGEND, NAVAHOS, PELICANOS
Type of Story	TRIBAL FICTION
Newbery Honor Book	FIELD, CALICO BUSH

On the back of this sheet, write why you think *Waterless Mountain* sounds interesting.

Name _____   Date _____

Young Fu of the Upper Yangtze by Elizabeth Foreman Lewis (1933)   *I–12*

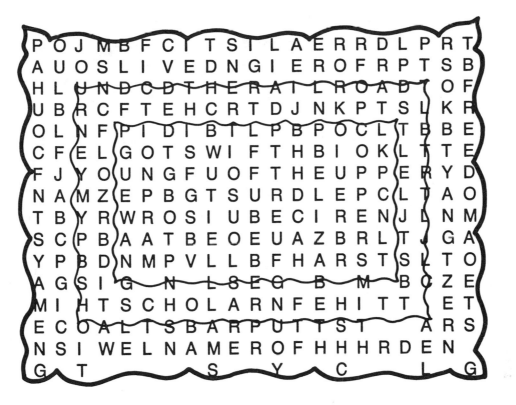

```
P O J M B F C I T S I L A E R R D L P R T
A U O S L I V E D N G I E R O F R P T S B
H L U N D C D T H E R A I L R O A D O F
U B R C F T E H C R T D J N K P T S L K R
O L N F P I D I B L P B P O C L T B B E
C F E L G O T S W I F T H B I O K L T E
F J Y O U N G F U O F T H E U P P E R Y D
N A M Z E P B G T S U R D L E P C L A O
T B Y R W R O S I U B E C I R E N J L N M
S C P B A A T B E O E U A Z B R L T J G A
Y P B D N M P V L L B F H A R S T S L T O
A G S I G N L S E G B M B C Z E
M I H T S C H O L A R N F E H I T T E E T
E C O A L T S B A R P U T T S T A R S
N S I W E L N A M E R O F H H H R D E N
G T S Y C L G
```

The words in the right-hand column may be found forward, backward, diagonally, horizontally, vertically, or a combination of these.

	Words to Find
Author	ELIZABETH FOREMAN LEWIS
Title	YOUNG FU OF THE UPPER YANGTZE
Main Character	YOUNG FU
Supporting Characters	DEN, SMALL LEI
Setting	CHINA
Words and Topics of Interest	FOREIGN DEVILS, APPRENTICE, JOURNEYMAN, COPPERSMITH, YA-MEN, GUILD, RICE
Type of Story	REALISTIC FICTION
Newbery Honor Book	SWIFT, THE RAILROAD TO FREEDOM

On the back of this sheet, write why you think *Young Fu of the Upper Yangtze* sounds interesting.

Invincible Louisa by Cornelia Meigs (1934)   *I–13*

```
            S N E D E K E R
            T E M E R S O N Y C M
       T W   Z B D G J L   N P S A
      D H   H E L I Z A B E T H J M Y
     P R E G T J B D C F E H Q R B T Z T
      T   F O R G O T T E N D A U G H T E R
    R D   B   A H F H J M P K L   B D C M F
    G J     N P T S V L O U I S A M B P J B
    B O   S   P W B Z X B L B P A Q L S R
   C I N V I N C I B L E L O U I S A Y R E T O
   B O L T R G E Q P Z X   T P S X B A H S V N
   T G N E W E N G L A N D B T X C P L M C P S
   P R L K N D M P B Q D R O C N O C D H Q O
    A T H N J E L K B O S T O N B F O E O T N
    P B D   N X B A H T R   B D P T T O L S
    H O S P I T A L S K E T C H E S T N L T
    Y T P I J A L K M O P T J P M R S B
     D C P L L G R I M S P R O G R E S S
      Q M L I T T L E W O M E N C F E
       P B S G I E M A I L E N R O C
       M F R U I T L A N D S
         J A N N A K B
```

The words in the right-hand column may be found forward, backward, diagonally, horizontally, vertically, or a combination of these.

Words to Find

Author	CORNELIA MEIGS
Title	<u>INVINCIBLE LOUISA</u>
Main Character	LOUISA MAY ALCOTT
Supporting Characters	BRONSON, ABBA, ANNA, ELIZABETH, MAY, EMERSON
Setting	NEW ENGLAND
Words and Topics of Interest	TEMPLE SCHOOL, FRUITLANDS, CONCORD, TRANSCENDENTALISM, PILGRIMS PROGRESS, LITTLE WOMEN
Type of Story	BIOGRAPHY
Newbery Honor Book	SNEDEKER, <u>THE FORGOTTEN DAUGHTER</u>

On the back of this sheet, write why you think *Invincible Louisa* sounds interesting.

Name _____   Date _____

Dobry **by Monica Shannon (1935)**

The words in the right-hand column may be found forward, backward, diagonally, horizontally, vertically, or a combination of these.

```
G           G
Y         H Y T
P F       I T B
S R       L B M N
C Y J     D M N T C
P B E A   R T C N L
N D F V   M N L I A
B U L G A R I A T Y R
O R C F N B C Y T S R
D P E A S A N T S R K T
S N O I T I D A R Y K M
R T P   D O B R Y K M O
L N E D A C F H T R O N
D A Y O N S K A T E S N I
P C L B R U T S Q H I C
L   J A M A L B T C A
    R T   R H O D A S
  F A M I L Y F C S H
    L G J P I T H A
    K R L W C Y Y A N
    X A N Q T P N N
    H N S I V N O
    T D U B O L N
    J F B H N L N
    B A L D T T
    N T R O Q B B
    X H T B A
    C E R R
    R T Y
```

Words to Find

Author	MONICA SHANNON
Title	DOBRY
Main Character	DOBRY
Supporting	
Characters	GRANDFATHER, RHODA, NEDA
Setting	BULGARIA
Words and Topics	
of Interest	JAMAL, CLAY, GYPSY BEAR, PEASANTS, TRADITIONS
Type of Story	FAMILY FICTION
Newbery Honor Book	HILDA VAN STOCKUM, DAY ON SKATES

On the back of this sheet, write why you think *Dobry* sounds interesting.

Name _____   Date _____

Caddie Woodlawn by Carol Ryrie Brink (1936)

The words in the right-hand column may be found forward, backward, diagonally, horizontally, vertically, or a combination of these.

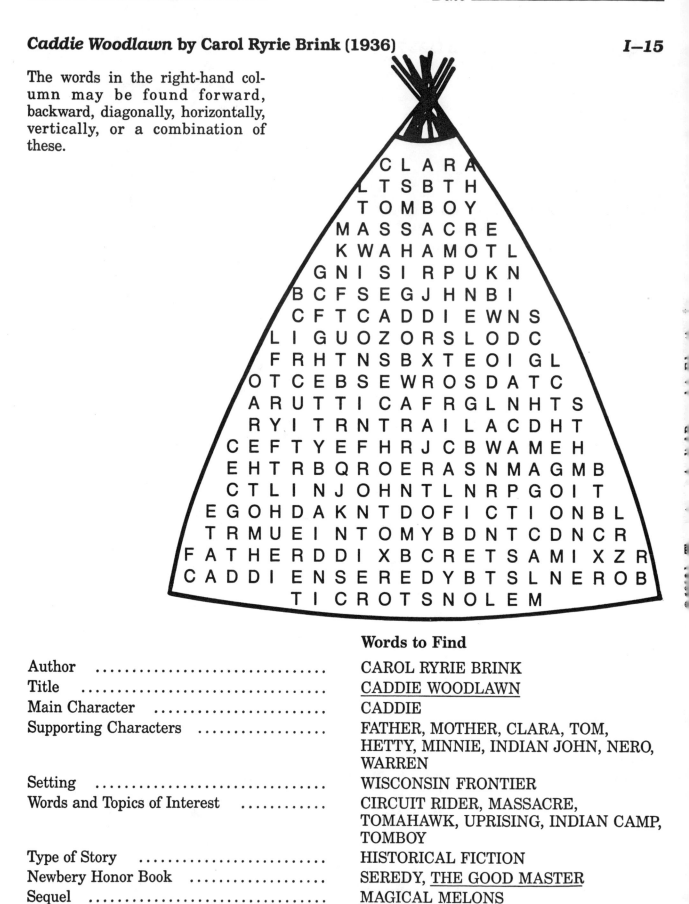

```
        C L A R A
        L T S B T H
        T O M B O Y
        M A S S A C R E
        K W A H A M O T L
        G N I S I R P U K N
        B C F S E G J H N B I
        C F T C A D D I E W N S
        L I G U O Z O R S L O D C
        F R H T N S B X T E O I G L
        O T C E B S E W R O S D A T C
        A R U T T I C A F R G L N H T S
        R Y I T R N T R A I L A C D H T
      C E F T Y E F H R J C B W A M E H
      E H T R B Q R O E R A S N M A G M B
      C T L I N J O H N T L N R P G O I T
      E G O H D A K N T D O F I C T I O N B L
      T R M U E I N T O M Y B D N T C D N C R
      F A T H E R D D I X B C R E T S A M I X Z R
      C A D D I E N S E R E D Y B T S L N E R O B
        T I C R O T S N O L E M
```

Words to Find

Author .... CAROL RYRIE BRINK

Title .... CADDIE WOODLAWN

Main Character .... CADDIE

Supporting Characters .... FATHER, MOTHER, CLARA, TOM, HETTY, MINNIE, INDIAN JOHN, NERO, WARREN

Setting .... WISCONSIN FRONTIER

Words and Topics of Interest .... CIRCUIT RIDER, MASSACRE, TOMAHAWK, UPRISING, INDIAN CAMP, TOMBOY

Type of Story .... HISTORICAL FICTION

Newbery Honor Book .... SEREDY, THE GOOD MASTER

Sequel .... MAGICAL MELONS

On the back of this sheet, write why you think *Caddie Woodlawn* sounds interesting.

Roller Skates by Ruth Sawyer (1937)   *I—16*

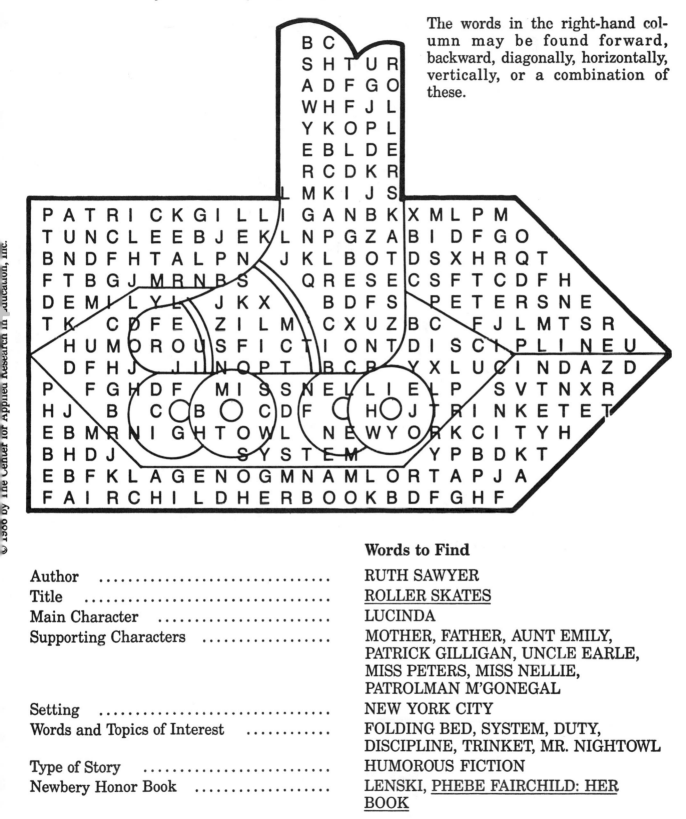

The words in the right-hand column may be found forward, backward, diagonally, horizontally, vertically, or a combination of these.

```
        B C
        S H T U R
        A D F G O
        W H F J L
        Y K O P L
        E B L D E
        R C D K R
        L M K I J S
P A T R I C K G I L L I G A N B K X M L P M
T U N C L E E B J E K L N P G Z A B I D F G O
B N D F H T A L P N J K L B O T D S X H R Q T
F T B G J M R N B S Q R E S E C S F T C D F H
D E M I L Y L J K X B D F S P E T E R S N E
T K C D F E Z I L M C X U Z B C F J L M T S R
H U M O R O U S F I C T I O N T D I S C I P L I N E U
D F H J J I N O P T B C R Y X L U C I N D A Z D
P F G H D F M I S S N E L L I E L P S V T N X R
H J B C B C D F H O J T R I N K E T E T
E B M R N I G H T O W L N E W Y O R K C I T Y H
B H D J S Y S T E M Y P B D K T
E B F K L A G E N O G M N A M L O R T A P J A
F A I R C H I L D H E R B O O K B D F G H F
```

Words to Find

Author   .... RUTH SAWYER
Title   .... <u>ROLLER SKATES</u>
Main Character .... LUCINDA
Supporting Characters .... MOTHER, FATHER, AUNT EMILY, PATRICK GILLIGAN, UNCLE EARLE, MISS PETERS, MISS NELLIE, PATROLMAN M'GONEGAL

Setting   .... NEW YORK CITY
Words and Topics of Interest .... FOLDING BED, SYSTEM, DUTY, DISCIPLINE, TRINKET, MR. NIGHTOWL
Type of Story   .... HUMOROUS FICTION
Newbery Honor Book .... LENSKI, <u>PHEBE FAIRCHILD: HER BOOK</u>

On the back of this sheet, write why you think *Roller Skates* sounds interesting.

Name _____   Date _____

The White Stag by Kate Seredy (1938)

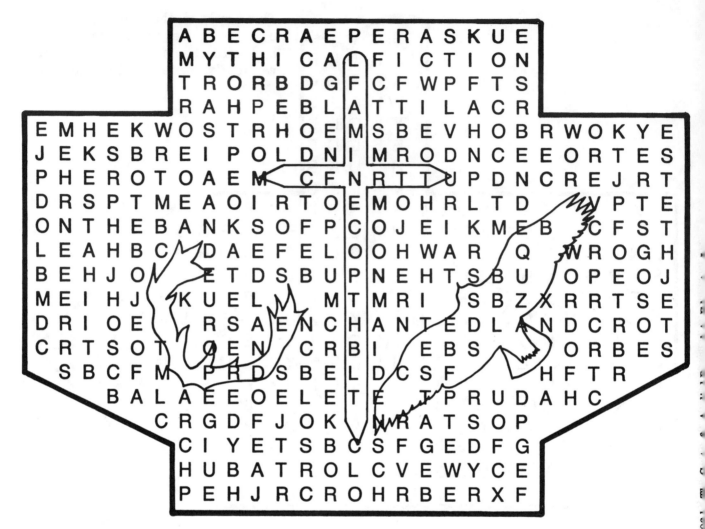

```
A B E C R A E P E R A S K U E
M Y T H I C A L F I C T I O N
T R O R B D G F C F W P F T S
R A H P E B L A T T I L A C R
E M H E K W O S T R H O E M S B E V H O B R W O K Y E
J E K S B R E I P O L D N I M R O D N C E E O R T E S
P H E R O T O A E M C F N R T T U P D N C R E J R T
D R S P T M E A O I R T O E M O H R L T D V P T E
O N T H E B A N K S O F P C O J E I K M E B C F S T
L E A H B C D A E F E L O O H W A R Q W R O G H
B E H J O E T D S B U P N E H T S B U O P E O J
M E I H J K U E L M T M R I S B Z X R R T S E
D R I O E R S A E N C H A N T E D L A N D C R O T
C R T S O T E N C R B I E B S O R B E S
S B C F M P R D S B E L D C S F H F T R
B A L A E E O E L E T E T P R U D A H C
C R G D F J O K N R A T S O P
C I Y E T S B C S F G E D F G
H U B A T R O L C V E W Y C E
P E H J R C R O H R B E R X F
```

The words in the right-hand column may be found forward, backward, diagonally, horizontally, vertically, or a combination of these.

Words to Find

Author	KATE SEREDY
Title	THE WHITE STAG
Main Character	HUNOR, MAGYAR
Supporting Characters	OLD NIMROD, DAMOS, BENDEQUZ, ATTILA
Setting	ASIA AND EUROPE
Words and Topics of Interest	EAGLE, PROMISED LAND, MOONMAIDENS, WAR, FAMINE, ENCHANTED LAND
Type of Story	MYTHICAL FICTION
Newbery Honor Book	WILDER, ON THE BANKS OF PLUM CREEK

On the back of this sheet, write why you think *The White Stag* sounds interesting.

Name _____   Date _____

Thimble Summer by Elizabeth Enright (1939)

The words in the right-hand column may be found forward,
backward, diagonally, horizontally,
vertically, or a combination of
these.

```
      B P L N
      C D G F J K L
    T B C F A T H E R
    O P A S R B C X M P Q
  A B C O R N P J K L M N D
  T H I M B L E S U M M E R V
  X P Y Z P M T N X Y P R B S T
  A F R F A M I L Y F I C T I O N
  O T J R H T U I H N Q I L M N L
  B H Y S T U V N F G T I M M Y I
  C J P W B C D D O N A L D R P B
  D K Q F C F G E H J X K Y T B R
A E X R A R R U N N I N G S U R A B
R C I T R O N E L L A H A U S E R Y
G R N H M R P J K T H T W V B D Y C
B C I F X M O T H E R R A M Q A X Y
S T S W Y B Z C F B H J Y X J H P Z
P S N I U G N E P S R E P P O P R M
B G O L T M R F R E E B O D Y S X Y
C J C D B L N T A H P C R T G B
J S R V X Z M P Q R X T H J L
E L I Z A B E T H E N R I G H T H
  W I X A T W A T E R B D J
```

Words to Find

Author ....   ELIZABETH ENRIGHT
Title ....   THIMBLE SUMMER
Main Character ....   GARNET LINDEN
Supporting Characters ....   FATHER, MOTHER, CITRONELLA
                                          HAUSER, JAY, DONALD, MR.
                                          FREEBODY

Setting ....   WISCONSIN
Words and Topics of Interest ....   FARM, TIMMY, LIBRARY, RUNNING
                                           AWAY
Type of Story ....   FAMILY FICTION
Newbery Honor Book ....   ATWATER, MR. POPPER'S PENGUINS

On the back of this sheet, write why you think *Thimble Summer* sounds interesting.

Daniel Boone by James Daugherty (1940)

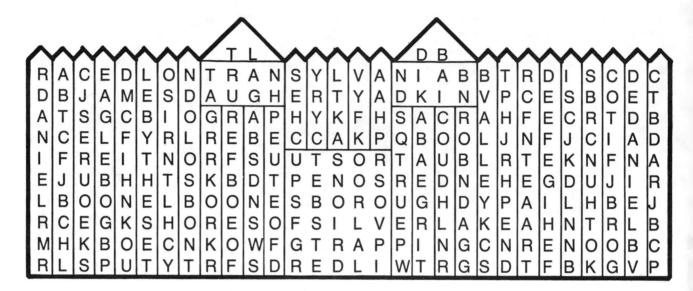

```
        T L                    D B
R A C E D L O N T R A N S Y L V A N I A B B T R D I S C D C
D B J A M E S D A U G H E R T Y A D K I N V P C E S B O E T
A T S G C B I O G R A P H Y K F H S A C R A H F E C R T D B
N C E L F Y R L R E B E C C A K P Q B O O L J N F J C I A D
I F R E I T N O R F S U U T S O R T A U B L R T E K N F A R
E J U B H H T S K B D T P E N O S R E D N E H E G D U J I R
L B O N E L B O O N E S B O R O U G H D Y P A I L H B E R J
R C E G K S H O R E S O F S I L V E R L A K E A H N T R L B
M H K B O E C N K O W F G T R A P P I N G C N R E N O O B C
R L S P U T Y T R F S D R E D L I W T R G S D T F B K G V P
```

The words in the right-hand column may be found forward, backward, diagonally, horizontally, vertically, or a combination of these.

Words to Find

Author	JAMES DAUGHERTY
Title	DANIEL BOONE
Main Character	DANIEL BOONE
Supporting Characters	REBECCA, JUDGE HENDERSON
Setting	U.S. FRONTIER
Words and Topics of Interest	YADKIN VALLEY, INDIANS, KENTUCKY, WILDERNESS, TRANSYLVANIA, TRAPPING
Type of Book	BIOGRAPHY
Newbery Honor Book	WILDER, BY THE SHORES OF SILVER LAKE

On the back of this sheet, write why you think *Daniel Boone* sounds interesting.

Name _____   Date _____

Call It Courage by Armstrong Sperry (1941)

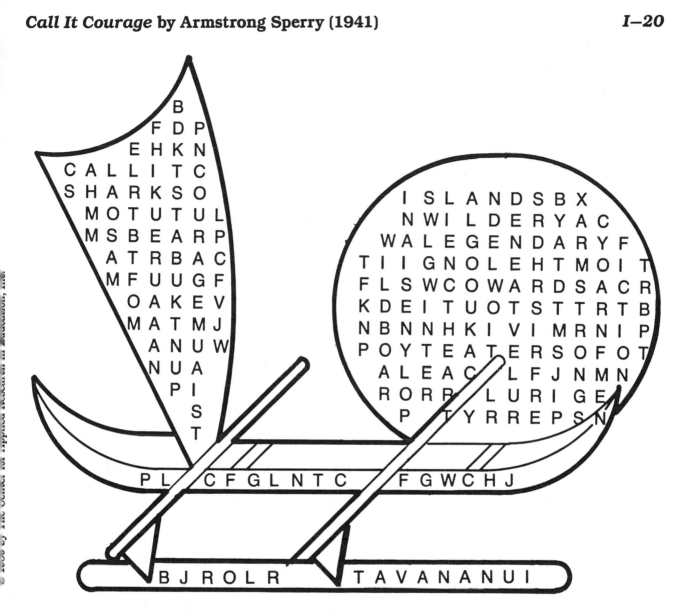

The words in the right-hand column may be found forward, backward, diagonally, horizontally, vertically, or a combination of these.

Words to Find

Author	ARMSTRONG SPERRY
Title	CALL IT COURAGE
Main Character	MAFATU
Supporting Characters	TAVANA NUI, URI, KIVI
Setting	POLYNESIAN ISLANDS
Words and Topics of Interest	COWARD, HIKUERU, MOANA, MAUI, SHARK, WILDBOAR, MOTU TABU, EATERS-OF-MEN
Type of Story	LEGENDARY FICTION
Newbery Honor Book	WILDER, THE LONG WINTER

On the back of this sheet, write why you think *Call It Courage* sounds interesting.

The words in the right-hand column may be found forward, backward, diagonally, horizontally, vertically, or a combination of these.

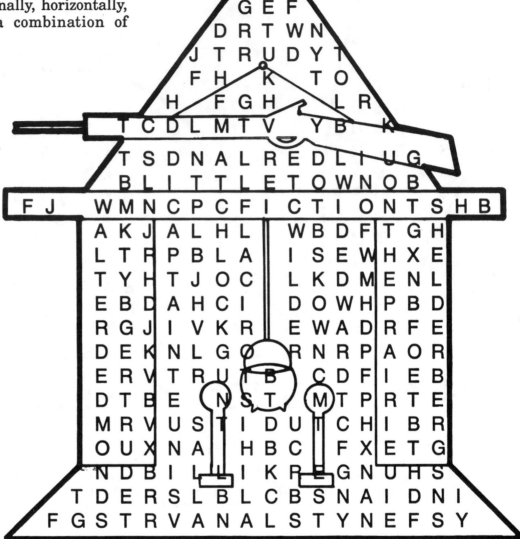

Words to Find

Author .... WALTER D. EDMONDS

Title .... THE MATCHLOCK GUN

Main Character .... EDWARD

Supporting Characters .... CAPTAIN TEUNIS VAN ALSTYNE, GERTRUDE, TRUDY

Setting .... NEW YORK

Words and Topics of Interest .... GUILDERLAND, HELDERBERGS, DUTCH, INDIANS, HUNGERKILL

Type of Story .... HISTORICAL FICTION

Newbery Honor Book .... WILDER, LITTLE TOWN ON THE PRAIRIE

On the back of this sheet, write why you think *The Matchlock Gun* sounds interesting.

Name _____   Date _____

Adam of the Road by Elizabeth Janet Gray (1943)   *I—22*

```
        A
      B A D A M O F T H E R O A D
      E D N A L G N E S L E V A R T
      J R O T M T H E M I D D L E M
      N I C K Q S P A Z H K E S O
      C T L O U   H A P C F T F
      L C I S U M A P B L   B E F
      I C J   N D R E H I J S A
      F L A C I R O T S I H E T
      T N L K O R H E   P F C
      R K B R F J D R E G N
      I R E X G A G K M V C F
      N G P O E N H A H A R P
      R O K R E T S P T Y L
      T R T T L O N D O N
      B H G R A Y S B T E
      E M I N S T R E L
      B E L R S C T
```

The words in the right-hand column may be found forward, backward, diagonally, horizontally, vertically, or a combination of these.

Words to Find

Author	ELIZABETH JANET GRAY
Title	ADAM OF THE ROAD
Main Character	ADAM QUARTERMAYNE
Supporting Characters	ROGER THE MINSTREL, NICK, PERKIN, JANKIN
Setting	ENGLAND
Words and Topics of Interest	HARP, TRAVELS, MUSIC, LONDON, OXFORD
Type of Book	HISTORICAL FICTION
Newbery Honor Book	ESTES, THE MIDDLE MOFFAT

On the back of this sheet, write why you think *Adam of the Road* sounds interesting.

Johnny Tremain by Esther Forbes (1944)   **I—23**

```
                                    B P C
    G M A G I C T E S B S I L V E R S M I T H
    O A P H I S T O R I C A L F E T Y L R M
    F H D E T E A P A R T Y U I T R L P T
    A S P T O H S B K J L N P F C U A J V
    N I A M E R T E T Y L N A H T A N O J
    C I L L A I H A P P R E N T I C E H T S P E
    S A R Y T R E B I L F O S N O S R N W Y O V
    N P M T L P R F O R B E S T N F G N O T S O B
                                    Y N R H D
                                    T R E M A I N     W
                                    P B U R N T S     A
                                    L A E O   P A L B A R
                                    S R     E F
                                    T
```

The words in the right-hand column may be found forward, backward, diagonally, horizontally, vertically, or a combination of these.

Words to Find

Author   ....   ESTHER FORBES

Title   ....   JOHNNY TREMAIN

Main Character ....   JONATHAN LYTE TREMAIN

Supporting Characters ....   MR. LAPHAM, DOVE, RAB, CILLA, MR. LYTE

Setting   ....   BOSTON

Words and Topics of Interest ....   APPRENTICE, SILVERSMITH, BURN, TEA PARTY, SONS OF LIBERTY, WAR

Type of Story   ....   HISTORICAL FICTION

Newbery Honor Book ....   SAUER, FOG MAGIC

On the back of this sheet, write why you think *Johnny Tremain* sounds interesting.

Name _____   Date _____

Rabbit Hill by Robert Lawson (1945)

The words in the right-hand column may be found forward, backward, diagonally, horizontally, vertically, or a combination of these.

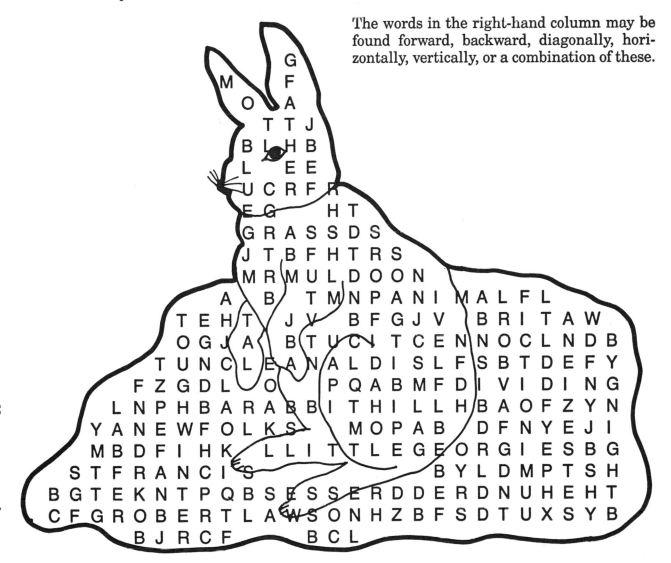

Words to Find

Author .... ROBERT LAWSON

Title .... RABBIT HILL

Main Character .... LITTLE GEORGIE

Supporting Characters .... MOTHER, FATHER, UNCLE ANALDIS, MAN, LADY, MR. MULDOON

Setting .... CONNECTICUT

Words and Topics of Interest .... DIVIDING NIGHT, ST. FRANCIS, BLUEGRASS, NEW FOLKS

Type of Story .... ANIMAL FICTION

Sequel .... THE TOUGH WINTER

Newbery Honor Book .... ESTES, THE HUNDRED DRESSES

On the back of this sheet, write why you think *Rabbit Hill* sounds interesting.

Name _____   Date _____

Strawberry Girl by Lois Lenski (1946)

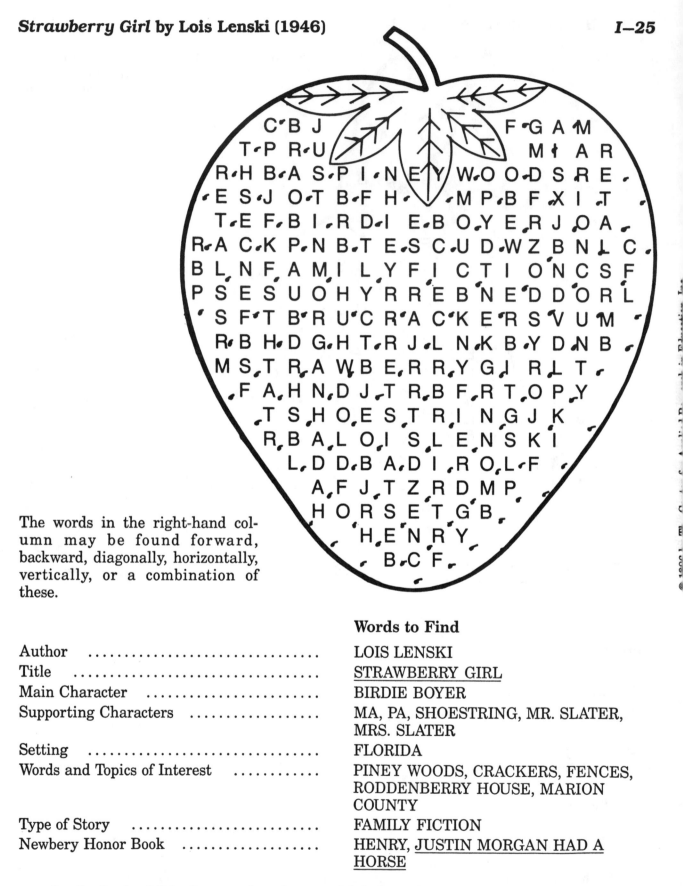

The words in the right-hand column may be found forward, backward, diagonally, horizontally, vertically, or a combination of these.

Words to Find

Author	LOIS LENSKI
Title	STRAWBERRY GIRL
Main Character	BIRDIE BOYER
Supporting Characters	MA, PA, SHOESTRING, MR. SLATER, MRS. SLATER
Setting	FLORIDA
Words and Topics of Interest	PINEY WOODS, CRACKERS, FENCES, RODDENBERRY HOUSE, MARION COUNTY
Type of Story	FAMILY FICTION
Newbery Honor Book	HENRY, JUSTIN MORGAN HAD A HORSE

On the back of this sheet, write why you think *Strawberry Girl* sounds interesting.

Miss Hickory by Carolyn Sherwin Bailey (1947)

The words in the right-hand column may be found forward, backward, diagonally, horizontally, vertically, or a combination of these.

```
        T R M
        O P R
        A L T
        H Q W
        T P I
        M V
        S T R B Y L Y
      S H I C K O R Y A B D E
B     J S P L A C E N P R E H E T
C U F   E F T L   T I D R N C T E V D Y B R Z
        F T P   M L T A U O W P B I G T L T
        C A R O L Y N S H E R W I N L
        E E R T E L P P A R O S H   A T
        S Q U I R R E L M P W R S B I V
        K N B M G U O R P T N L M T L Z
        T R I L B N Y S A T N A F E W B R T
        W S L H J N H K P B D C Y   I O W
        S C I O N I N P A B   K N S O N
        H I C K O R Y G       T T R R P
        C F E                 E O C T
                              R N O
```

Words to Find

Author	CAROLYN SHERWIN BAILEY
Title	<u>MISS HICKORY</u>
Main Character	MISS HICKORY
Supporting Characters	CROW, MR. T. WILLARD-BROWN, SQUIRREL
Setting	NEW HAMPSHIRE
Words and Topics of Interest	OLD PLACE, BOSTON, WINTER, SCION, APPLETREE
Type of Book	FANTASY
Newbery Honor Book	BUFF, <u>BIG TREE</u>

On the back of this sheet, write why you think *Miss Hickory* sounds interesting.

Name _____   Date _____

The Twenty-One Balloons by William Pene DuBois (1948)

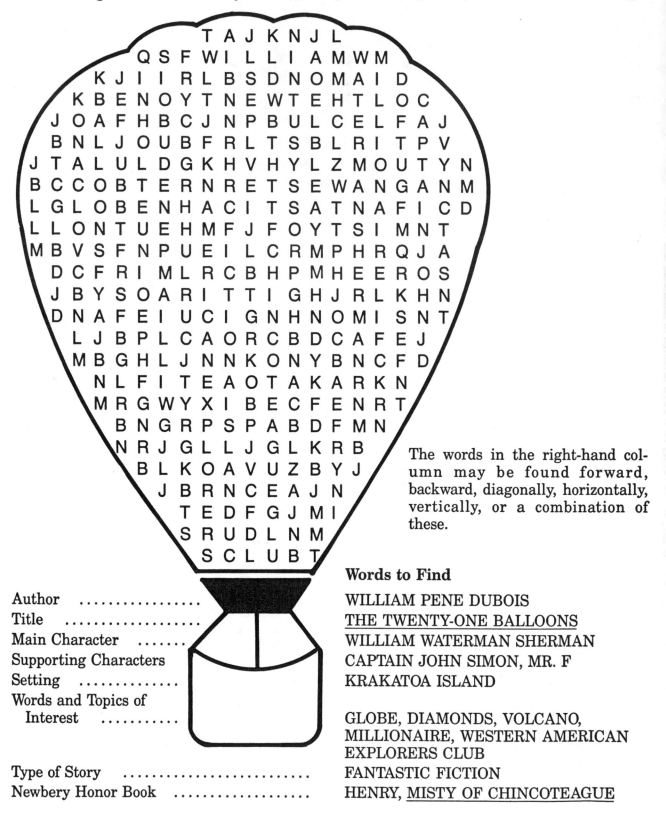

```
              T A J K N J L
            Q S F WI L L I A M W M
          K J I I R L B S D N O M A I D
          K B E N O Y T N E W T E H T L O C
        J O A F H B C J N P B U L C E L F A J
        B N L J O U B F R L T S B L R I T P V
      J T A L U L D G K H V H Y L Z M O U T Y N
      B C C O B T E R N R E T S E W A N G A N M
      L G L O B E N H A C I T S A T N A F I C D
      L L O N T U E H M F J F O Y T S I M N T
    M B V S F N P U E I L C R M P H R Q J A
      D C F R I M L R C B H P M H E E R O S
      J B Y S O A R I T T I G H J R L K H N
      D N A F E I U C I G N H N O M I S N T
        L J B P L C A O R C B D C A F E J
        M B G H L J N N K O N Y B N C F D
          N L F I T E A O T A K A R K N
          M R G W Y X I B E C F E N R T
            B N G R P S P A B D F M N
            N R J G L L J G L K R B
              B L K O A V U Z B Y J
              J B R N C E A J N
                T E D F G J M I
                S R U D L N M
                S C L U B T
```

The words in the right-hand column may be found forward, backward, diagonally, horizontally, vertically, or a combination of these.

Words to Find

Author ....

Title ....

Main Character ....

Supporting Characters

Setting ....

Words and Topics of
   Interest ....

Type of Story ....

Newbery Honor Book ....

WILLIAM PENE DUBOIS

THE TWENTY-ONE BALLOONS

WILLIAM WATERMAN SHERMAN

CAPTAIN JOHN SIMON, MR. F

KRAKATOA ISLAND

GLOBE, DIAMONDS, VOLCANO,
MILLIONAIRE, WESTERN AMERICAN
EXPLORERS CLUB

FANTASTIC FICTION

HENRY, MISTY OF CHINCOTEAGUE

On the back of this sheet, write why you think *The Twenty-One Balloons* sounds interesting.

King of the Wind by Marguerite Henry (1949)

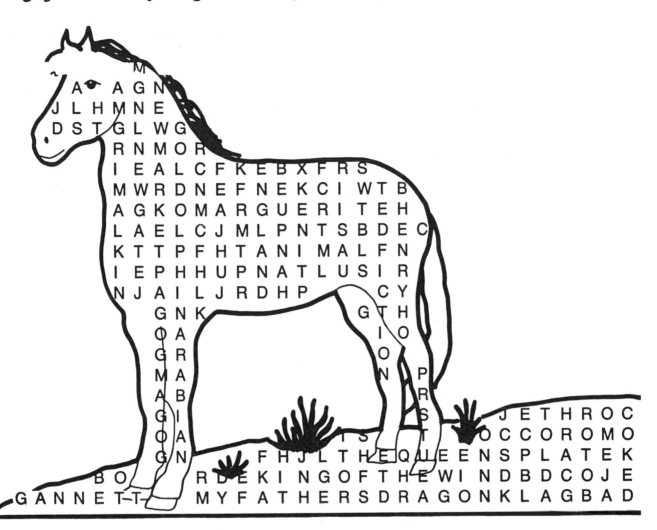

The words in the right-hand column may be found forward, backward, diagonally, horizontally, vertically, or a combination of these.

Words to Find

Author	MARGUERITE HENRY
Title	<u>KING OF THE WIND</u>
Main Character	SHAM
Supporting Characters	AGBA, JETHRO COKE, GRIMALKIN
Setting	MOROCCO, ENGLAND
Words and Topics of Interest	SULTAN, NEWGATE JAIL, GOG MAGOG, NEWMARKET, WICKEN FEN, THE QUEEN'S PLATE, GOLDOLPHIN ARABIAN
Type of Story	ANIMAL FICTION
Newbery Honor Book	GANNETT, <u>MY FATHER'S DRAGON</u>

On the back of this sheet, write why you think *King of the Wind* sounds interesting.

Name _____   Date _____

The Door in the Wall by Marguerite de Angeli (1950)

```
F  B  D  C  S  G  J  K  O  P  T     S  N  U  H     J  B  D  G  E  O  R  G  E  W  C  F
I  O  J  R  L  H  I  S  T  O  R  I  C  A  L  C  S     R  T  B  O  L  T  S  B  A  E  T
J  A  S  U  B  T  P  R  Y     M  Y  O  Z  F  B  I  D     F  G  H  A  K  L  N  S  P  L
R  O  B  T  G  H  J  M  O  P  A  B  T  S  I  Q  R  T  L  U  B  X  Y  R  E  T  H  O  N
P  S  D  C  E  F  I  L  P  Q  R  A  T  C  C  H  P  B  T  J  P  L  N  D  K  B  I  T  J
H  T  P  H  O  R  J  O  H  N  G  O  I  N  T  H  E  W  Y  N  D  R  T  B  U  S  N  P  C
O  B  J  E  F  E  C  P  O  V  U  B  S  O  I  L  T  B  R  O  T  H  E  R  L  T  G  B  D
S  T  U  S  T  M  A  R  K  S  E  V  H  B  O  S  E  I  T  U  D  F  I  K  N  P  T  S  F
K  T  S  B  R  T  O  U  J  S  R  A  W  K  N  L  R  I  S  B  A  E  O  U  K  L  O  B  P
L  P  C  E  G  N  J  H  G  N  I  V  R  A  C  D  O  O  W  T  S  W  I  M  M  I  N  G  C
C  O  H  J  I  N  P  R  U  S  T  H  E  D  O  O  R  I  N  T  H  E  W  A  L  L  M  H  B
A  J  O  B  C  F  E  L  T  W  E  L  S  H  A  T  T  A  C  K  B  O  T  S  J  K  T  N  R
B  T  O  X  F  O  R  D  E  R  D  E  A  N  G  E  L  I  C  O  L  H  R  Y  T  A  K  J  E
G  R  L  O  U  F  X  T  J  P  U  V  T  R  O  K  H  J  E  N  G  L  A  N  D  R  S  B  A
```

The words in the right-hand column may be found forward, backward, diagonally, horizontally, vertically, or a combination of these.

	Words to Find
Author	MARGUERITE DE ANGELI
Title	THE DOOR IN THE WALL
Main Character	ROBIN
Supporting Characters	BROTHER LUKE, JOHN-GO-IN-THE-WYND, D'ATH, SIR PETER
Setting	ENGLAND
Words and Topics of Interest	ST. MARKS, WOODCARVING, SWIMMING, OXFORD, SCOTTISH WARS, CRUTCHES
Type of Story	HISTORICAL FICTION
Newbery Honor Book	FOSTER, GEORGE WASHINGTON

On the back of this sheet, write why you think *The Door in the Wall* sounds interesting.

Name _____ Date _____

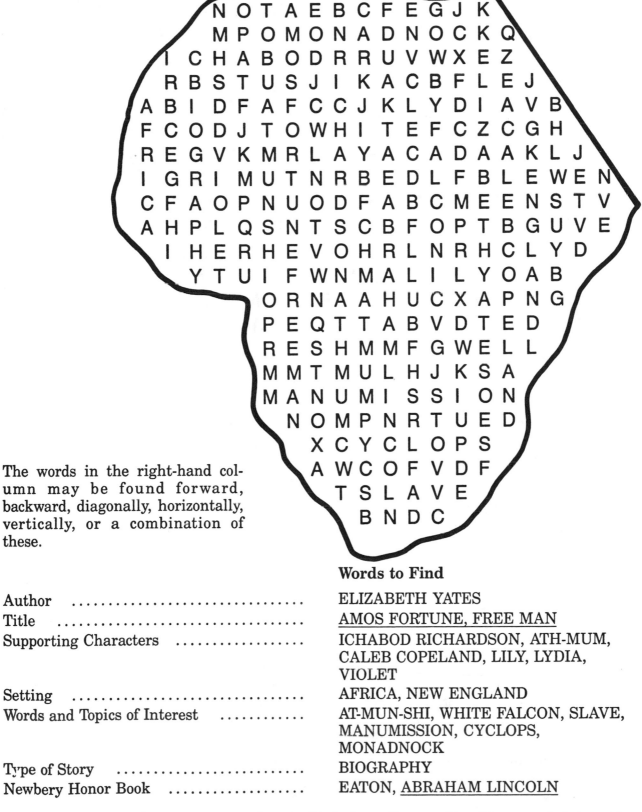

The words in the right-hand column may be found forward, backward, diagonally, horizontally, vertically, or a combination of these.

Words to Find

Author .... ELIZABETH YATES

Title .... AMOS FORTUNE, FREE MAN

Supporting Characters .... ICHABOD RICHARDSON, ATH-MUM, CALEB COPELAND, LILY, LYDIA, VIOLET

Setting .... AFRICA, NEW ENGLAND

Words and Topics of Interest .... AT-MUN-SHI, WHITE FALCON, SLAVE, MANUMISSION, CYCLOPS, MONADNOCK

Type of Story .... BIOGRAPHY

Newbery Honor Book .... EATON, ABRAHAM LINCOLN

On the back of this sheet, write why you think *Amos Fortune, Free Man* sounds interesting.

Name _____   Date _____

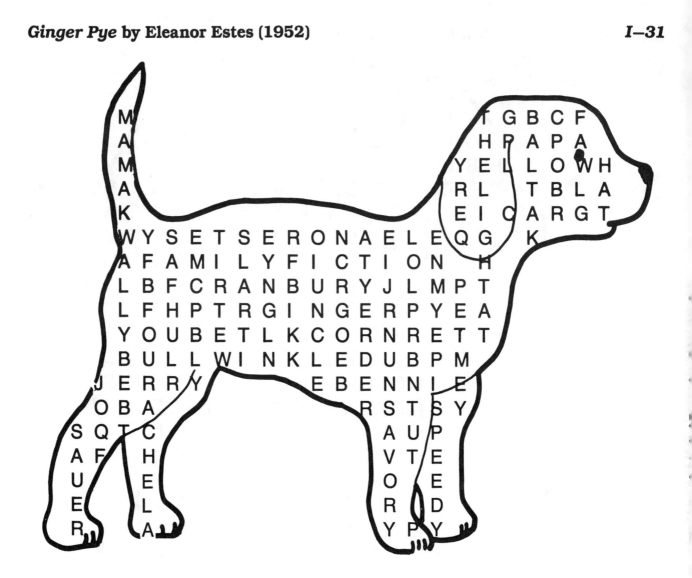

The words in the right-hand column may be found forward, backward, diagonally, horizontally, vertically, or a combination of these.

Words to Find

Author	ELEANOR ESTES
Title	GINGER PYE
Main Character	JERRY
Supporting Characters	RACHEL, MAMA, PAPA, GRACIE, UNCLE BENNIE
Setting	CRANBURY
Words and Topics of Interest	SPEEDY, YOU BET, YELLOW HAT, UNSAVORY, WALLY BULLWINKLE
Type of Story	FAMILY FICTION
Newbery Honor Book	SAUER, THE LIGHT AT TERN ROCK

On the back of this sheet, write why you think *Ginger Pye* sounds interesting.

Secret of the Andes by Ann Nolan Clark (1953)

The words in the right-hand column may be found forward, backward, diagonally, horizontally, vertically, or a combination of these.

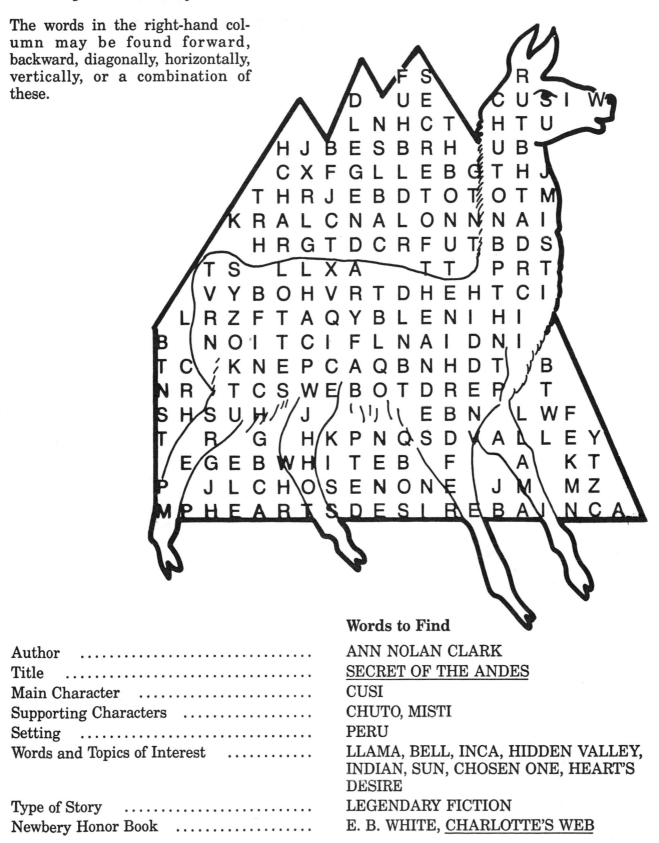

Words to Find

Author	ANN NOLAN CLARK
Title	<u>SECRET OF THE ANDES</u>
Main Character	CUSI
Supporting Characters	CHUTO, MISTI
Setting	PERU
Words and Topics of Interest	LLAMA, BELL, INCA, HIDDEN VALLEY, INDIAN, SUN, CHOSEN ONE, HEART'S DESIRE
Type of Story	LEGENDARY FICTION
Newbery Honor Book	E. B. WHITE, <u>CHARLOTTE'S WEB</u>

On the back of this sheet, write why you think *Secret of the Andes* sounds interesting.

Name _____   Date _____

And Now Miguel by Joseph Krumgold (1954)

The words in the right-hand column may be found forward, backward, diagonally, horizontally, vertically, or a combination of these.

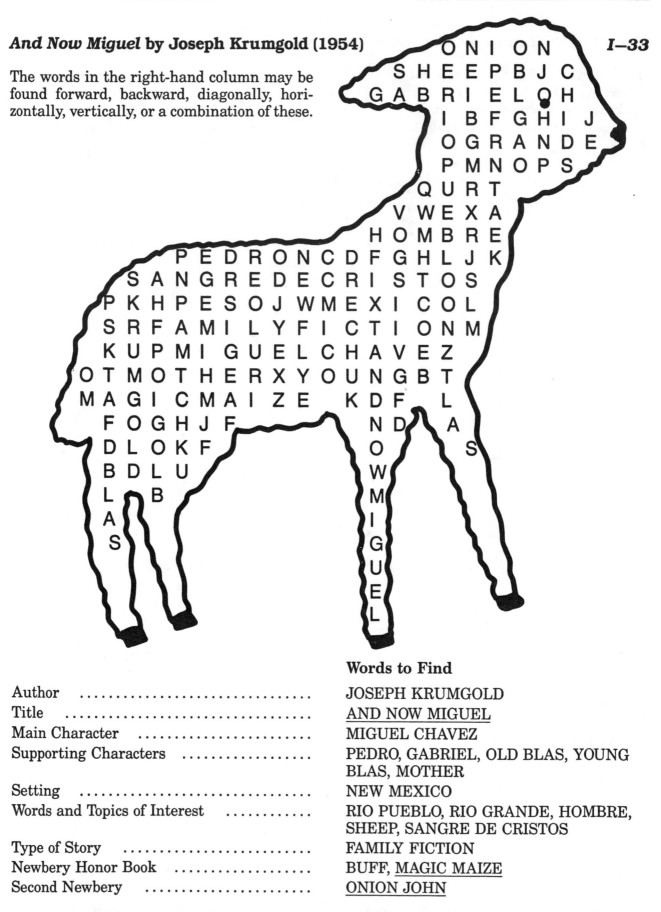

Words to Find

Author	JOSEPH KRUMGOLD
Title	AND NOW MIGUEL
Main Character	MIGUEL CHAVEZ
Supporting Characters	PEDRO, GABRIEL, OLD BLAS, YOUNG BLAS, MOTHER
Setting	NEW MEXICO
Words and Topics of Interest	RIO PUEBLO, RIO GRANDE, HOMBRE, SHEEP, SANGRE DE CRISTOS
Type of Story	FAMILY FICTION
Newbery Honor Book	BUFF, MAGIC MAIZE
Second Newbery	ONION JOHN

On the back of this sheet, write why you think *And Now Miguel* sounds interesting.

The Wheel on the School by Meindert DeJong (1955)

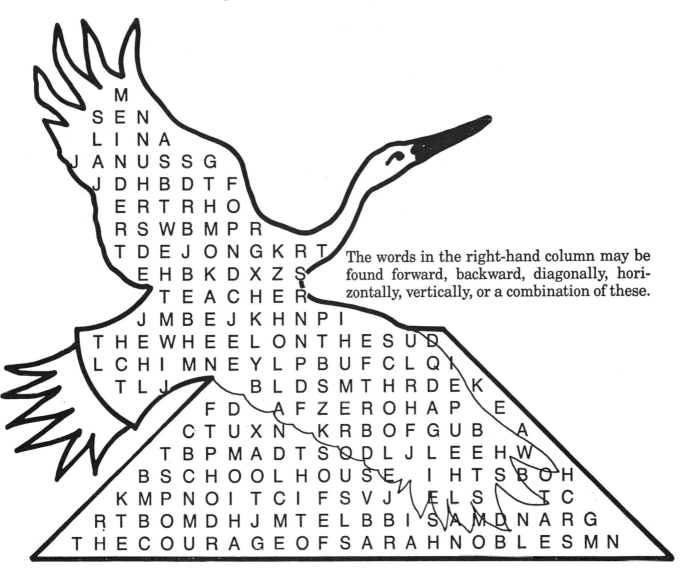

The words in the right-hand column may be found forward, backward, diagonally, horizontally, vertically, or a combination of these.

Words to Find

Author	MEINDERT DEJONG
Title	THE WHEEL ON THE SCHOOL
Main Character	LINA
Supporting Characters	TEACHER, JANUS, GRANDMA SIBBLE
Setting	HOLLAND
Words and Topics of Interest	SCHOOLHOUSE, STORKS, DIKE, CHIMNEY, WHEEL
Type of Story	HUMOROUS FICTION
Newbery Honor Book	DAGLIESH, THE COURAGE OF SARAH NOBLE

On the back of this sheet, write why you think *The Wheel on the School* sounds interesting.

Carry On, Mr. Bowditch by Jean Lee Latham (1956)

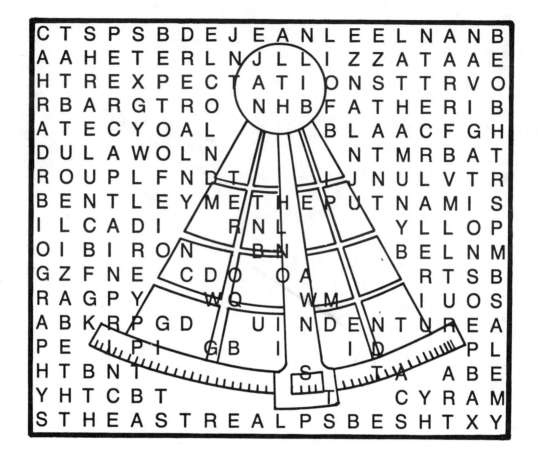

```
C T S P S B D E J E A N L E E L N A N B
A A H E T E R L N J L L I Z Z A T A A E
H T R E X P E C T A T I O N S T T R V O
R B A R G T R O N H B F A T H E R I B
A T E C Y O A L B L A A C F G H
D U L A W O L N N T M R B A T
R O U P L F N D T J N U L V T R
B E N T L E Y M E T H E P U T N A M I S
I L C A D I R N L Y L L O P
O I B I R O N B N B E L N M
G Z F N E C D O O A R T S B
R A G P Y W Q W M I U O S
A B K R P G D U I N D E N T U R E A
P E L J P I G B I I O P L
H T B N I S T A A B E
Y H T C B T T C Y R A M
S T H E A S T R E A L P S B E S H T X Y
```

The words in the right-hand column may be found forward, backward, diagonally, horizontally, vertically, or a combination of these.

Words to Find

Author	....	JEAN LEE LATHAM
Title	....	CARRY ON, MR. BOWDITCH
Main Character	....	NATHANIEL BOWDITCH
Supporting Characters	....	FATHER, LIZZA, MARY, POLLY, ELIZABETH, CAPTAIN PRINCE, DR. BENTLEY
Setting	....	SALEM
Words and Topics of Interest	....	EXPECTATIONS, INDENTURE, SEXTANT, THE ASTREA, THE PUTNAM, NAVIGATION
Type of Story	....	BIOGRAPHY
Newbery Honor Book	....	LINDQUIST, THE GOLDEN NAME DAY

On the back of this sheet, write why you think _Carry On, Mr. Bowditch_ sounds interesting.

Name _____   Date _____

Miracles on Maple Hill by Virginia Sorensen (1957)

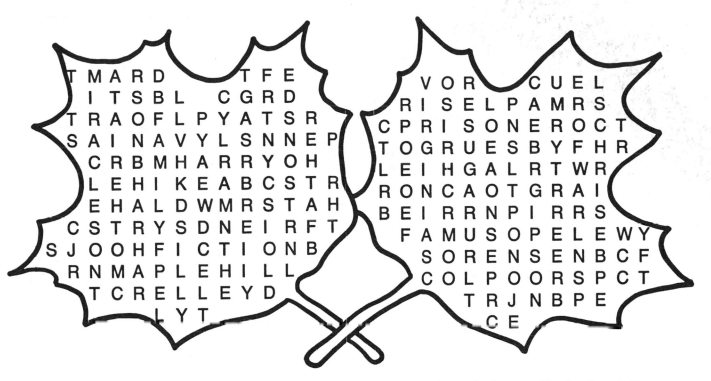

The words in the right-hand column may be found forward, backward, diagonally, horizontally, vertically, or a combination of these.

Words to Find

Author	VIRGINIA SORENSEN
Title	MIRACLES ON MAPLE HILL
Main Character	MARLY
Supporting Characters	MOTHER, FATHER, JOE, HARRY, MR. CHRIS, MRS. CHRIS
Setting	PENNSYLVANIA
Words and Topics of Interest	COUNTRY, PRISONER OF WAR, FRIENDS, MAPLE SUGAR
Type of Story	FAMILY FICTION
Newbery Honor Book	GIPSON, OLD YELLER

On the back of this sheet, write why you think *Miracles on Maple Hill* sounds interesting.

Name _____   Date _____

Rifles for Watie by Harold Keith (1958)

```
A T S B R K J E F F E R S O N D     G O N E A W A Y L A K E Y
H P B M N L T Q B A D T I J R A     A L A C I R O T S I H D B
A V T R S B D H K N P R L T O V     F U R T G E N E R A L
R E P E A T I N G R I F L E S I     M I X N D T B A D W
O W Y T S A F E J M D T B C J S     I C T I B R L T T A
L R L W N P M S R I F L E S F B     D T O R O T C X Y B T
D A Q R B F N N S V A L R F O U     D I S B Z N P L M N I
K A N S A S V O L U N T E E R S     L O B C I V I L W A R E
E E O N T R L A V X Z B Y A W S     E N H A K M R T B T
I L R J L K B H K D M N B F A E     W E S T F B F E E R
T R J K U O L B A B B I T T T Y     B P D X Y D R B Z
H D F E C K V D C E T F L M I T     Q A L N T H G I R N E T
Q A R Z Y W A S H B O U R N E B     C R B T H K B R L Z L
```

The words in the right-hand column may be found forward, backward, diagonally, horizontally, vertically, or a combination of these.

Words to Find

Author	HAROLD KEITH
Title	RIFLES FOR WATIE
Main Character	JEFFERSON DAVIS BUSSEY
Supporting Characters	CAPTAIN CLARDY, NOAH BABBITT, LUCY WASHBOURNE
Setting	MIDDLE WEST
Words and Topics of Interest	GENERAL WATIE, CIVIL WAR, REBEL, UNION, REPEATING RIFLES
Type of Story	HISTORICAL FICTION
Newbery Honor Book	ENRIGHT, GONE-AWAY LAKE

On the back of this sheet, write why you think *Rifles for Watie* sounds interesting.

Name _____ Date _____

The Witch of Blackbird Pond by Elizabeth George Speare (1959) I—38

The words in the right-hand column may be found forward, backward, diagonally, horizontally, vertically, or a combination of these.

B C A F G
K I T T Y L E R L
H J E L I Z A B E T H G
M N O T P Q B U C S T U E V
T H E F H K A N O S W T O X C
A B A E S R T N A I A R H J
J M W V B R N Y D T G S R L
U I I H L A A E B O K E F G S
L D N L T I M D C C R W J S K J L
N I O Y C S O H T O T U P P E R
P T R U H T S E I O S H E V Z P
H T U O O L L C K R B A C D E
Y X P D F N N A U F H A R V R S
C R T O E B I O V U T R I V E R T
R S K L R L C O N N E C T I C U T
T A P T A A M A H B Y X C D
M H H C L A E J K L M N O
L T H E B A E K F I C T I O N
S T J R C B B R L F W
T V R O U R I S L K
J N N R I R T I C
I Z U D D U W A
S E N G P N
B C E O A V
O L Y N T V
W E Z D E A T O N
M A T T H E W
C A R L S O N
W I T C H

Words to Find

Author ..... ELIZABETH GEORGE SPEARE
Title .. THE WITCH OF BLACKBIRD POND
Main Character .... KIT TYLER
Supporting Characters .... AUNT RACHEL, UNCLE
   MATTHEW, MARCY,
   JUDITH, WIDOW
   TUPPER, NAT EATON
Setting .... CONNECTICUT
Words and Topics of Interest ... BARBADOS, WITCH, SAYBROOK,
   CONNECTICUT RIVER
Type of Story .... HISTORICAL FICTION
Newbery Honor Book .... CARLSON, THE FAMILY UNDER THE
   BRIDGE
Second Newbery .... THE BRONZE BOW

On the back of this sheet, write why you think *The Witch of Blackbird Pond* sounds interesting.

Name _____ **Date** _____

Onion John by Joseph Krumgold (1960)

The words in the right-hand column may be found forward, backward, diagonally, horizontally, vertically, or a combination of these.

```
          T C
          S H
          C H P
          S C A F
      U E E L H L
    P R L H B L E R R
    B Y D C F J O S E P H K
  C D D B E O L W S H C P R P
O N I O N J S F E I T S Q U R
A F B D P O E F E A A C C M E L
N P B C F H F G N N F E H G A K
D U M P L N L L I H G M N O L R
N U N I T E D S T A T E S L I O
O P R T S U L V M N Y A X D S T
W Z P R T O L M L O C F P G T A
M I G U E L A H K N J L N O I R
P T R E D G D L K I M B U L C Y
  N P J E T N R N O I T C I F
  S H P S E R E N I T Y L
  T B T D K L N J O H N
  B A T H R O B E
      P T
```

Words to Find

Author .... JOSEPH KRUMGOLD
Title .... <u>ONION JOHN</u>
Main Character .... ANDY RUSCH
Supporting Characters .... ONION JOHN, FATHER
Setting .... UNITED STATES
Words and Topics of Interest .... SERENITY, HESSIAN HILL, ROTARY CLUB, DUMP, FIDDLE, BATHROBE, HALLOWEEN
Type of Story .... REALISTIC FICTION
Newbery Honor Book .... KENDALL, <u>THE GAMMAGE CUP</u>
Second Newbery .... <u>AND NOW MIGUEL</u>

On the back of this sheet, write why you think *Onion John* sounds interesting.

Name _____   Date _____

Island of the Blue Dolphins by Scott O'Dell (1961)

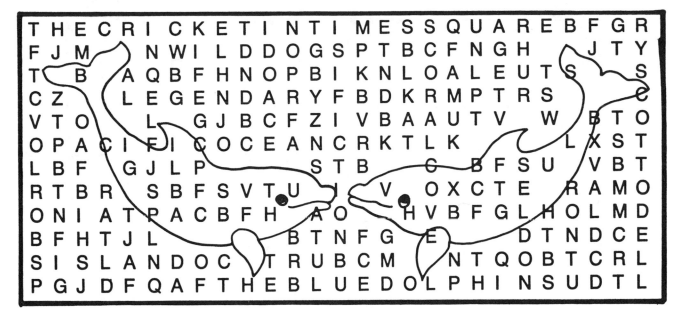

```
T H E C R I C K E T I N T I M E S S Q U A R E B F G R
F J M   N W I L D D O G S P T B C F N G H     J T Y
T   B   A Q B F H N O P B I K N L O A L E U T S   S
C Z     L E G E N D A R Y F B D K R M P T R S     C
V T O     L G J B C F Z I V B A A U T V   W   B T O
O P A C I F I C O C E A N C R K T L K       L X S T
L B F   G J L P     S T B   C   B F S U   V B T
R T B R   S B F S V T U   V   O X C T E   R A M O
O N I A T P A C B F H   A O   H V B F G L H O L M D
B F H T J L     B T N F G   E       D T N D C E
S I S L A N D O C T R U B C M   N T Q O B T C R L
P G J D F Q A F T H E B L U E D O L P H I N S U D T L
```

The words in the right-hand column may be found forward, backward, diagonally, horizontally, vertically, or a combination of these.

Author ....   **Words to Find**

Author ....   SCOTT O'DELL

Title ....   ISLAND OF THE BLUE DOLPHINS

Main Character ....   KARANA

Supporting Characters ....   RAMO, CAPTAIN ORLOV, RONTU

Setting ....   PACIFIC OCEAN

Words and Topics of Interest ....   ALEUTS, CORAL COVE, WILD DOGS

Type of Story ....   LEGENDARY FICTION

Newbery Honor Book ....   SELDON, THE CRICKET IN TIMES
SQUARE

On the back of this sheet, write why you think *Island of the Blue Dolphins* sounds interesting.

Name _____   Date _____

The Bronze Bow by Elizabeth George Speare (1962)

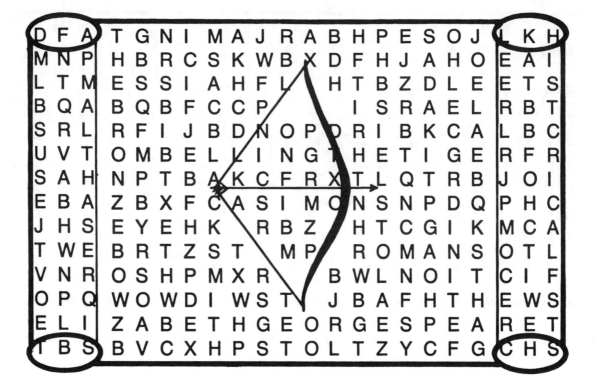

The words in the right-hand column may be found forward, backward, diagonally, horizontally, vertically, or a combination of these.

Words to Find

Author	ELIZABETH GEORGE SPEARE
Title	THE BRONZE BOW
Main Character	JOSEPH BAR JAMIN
Supporting Characters	LEAH, ROSH, JOEL, MALTHASE, SIMON
Setting	ISRAEL
Words and Topics of Interest	ROMANS, ZEALOTS, BLACKSMITH, MESSIAH, JESUS
Type of Story	HISTORICAL FICTION
Newbery Honor Book	STOLTZ, BELLING THE TIGER
Second Newbery	THE WITCH OF BLACKBIRD POND

On the back of this sheet, write why you think *The Bronze Bow* sounds interesting.

A Wrinkle in Time by Madeleine L'Engle (1963)   **I—42**

```
M D B J M P I T A R H C H A R L E S W A L L A C E Q T P
A W R I N K L E I N T I M E B R P F G K N P T B D R B O
D P T C N F H S G C J L O T F D F E T R B S Q T H L K W
E T R F O J P S N A M B S G V X L M B T C O O L I D G E
L D O B I R T E S L M E N O F A T H E N S B T R C E F R
E G O H S J P R Z V E B P T N O I T C I F E C N E I C S
I R D R N R B A E I G K R H C I H W S R M S W H O R O
N B E A E F T C R N M P B T A R J R N R K R J A U H F
L P T N I C Q S V K R S H A A I L A U H W R G T V E W A
E T N R D R B H D E R B K R Z L R B K N H Y O H U R H R
N H I C H P D K Y E Y R L F O B O D B C A J U L N S T K
G J D X T H N R B F T Z F A T H E R P X T R A Q L P R N
L B N V F I H S D E B G M H Z M V C E S T Y I N A B E
E P I B I J T A X C F J K T R B E F T H I R V O K C T S
A S W I F T L Y T I L T I N G P L A N E T E B J V E R S
```

The words in the right-hand column may be found forward, backward, diagonally, horizontally, vertically, or a combination of these.

Words to Find

Author .... MADELEINE L'ENGLE

Title .... A WRINKLE IN TIME

Main Character .... MEG MURRY

Supporting Characters .... CHARLES WALLACE, FATHER, CALVIN O'KEEFE

Setting .... OUTER SPACE

Words and Topics of Interest .... MRS. WHATSIT, MRS. WHO, TESSERACT, EVIL, MRS. WHICH, CAMAZOTZ, BRAIN, POWERS OF DARKNESS, IT

Type of Story .... SCIENCE FICTION

Newbery Honor Book .... COOLIDGE, MEN OF ATHENS

Sequels .... WIND IN THE DOOR, A SWIFTLY TILTING PLANET

On the back of this sheet, write why you think *A Wrinkle in Time* sounds interesting.

It's Like This, Cat by Emily Neville (1964)

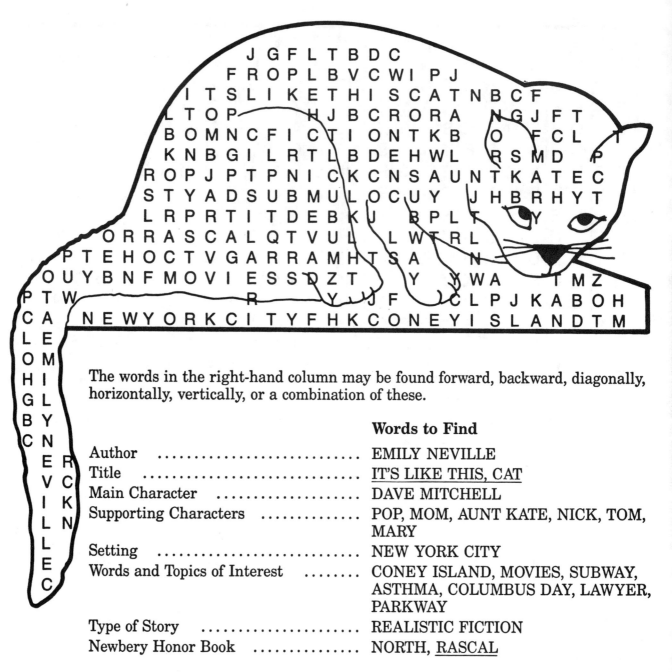

The words in the right-hand column may be found forward, backward, diagonally, horizontally, vertically, or a combination of these.

Words to Find

Author .... EMILY NEVILLE

Title .... IT'S LIKE THIS, CAT

Main Character .... DAVE MITCHELL

Supporting Characters .... POP, MOM, AUNT KATE, NICK, TOM, MARY

Setting .... NEW YORK CITY

Words and Topics of Interest .... CONEY ISLAND, MOVIES, SUBWAY, ASTHMA, COLUMBUS DAY, LAWYER, PARKWAY

Type of Story .... REALISTIC FICTION

Newbery Honor Book .... NORTH, RASCAL

On the back of this sheet, write why you think *It's Like This, Cat* sounds interesting.

Shadow of a Bull **by Maia Wojciechowska (1965)**

The words in the right-hand column may be found forward, backward, diagonally, horizontally, vertically, or a combination of these.

Words to Find

Author	MAIA WOJCIECHOWSKA
Title	SHADOW OF A BULL
Main Character	MANOLO OLIVAR
Supporting Characters	JUAN OLIVAR, COUNT DE LA CASA, OLD DOCTOR, JUAN GARCIA
Setting	SPAIN
Words and Topics of Interest	BULL, BULLFIGHT, MULETA, MATADOR, FEAR, FAMOUS
Type of Story	REALISTIC FICTION
Newbery Honor Book	HUNT, ACROSS FIVE APRILS

On the back of this sheet, write why you think *Shadow of a Bull* sounds interesting.

Name _____   Date _____

I, Juan de Pareja by Elizabeth Borton de Treviño (1966)

The words in the right-hand column may be found forward, backward, diagonally, horizontally, vertically, or a combination of these.

```
          T J A B C
          T S E V I L L E R
        G Y T L A Y O L P F F R
      B K N A   E H L T T Y R D A
      L A C I R O T S I H B R E J T R
      F R Y T O R E T S A M P E L S B T
      I T T H E K I N G P T R D B M S B
      C O R E D N A X E L A G O H I N T
      T L K B J T O B C P E H M K S P T J
      I O E L I Z A B E T H B O R T O N D
      O M B A E M A D R I D R E S R P D E
      N E R C T R N P O H T O P O E B E T
      L G H K C A L D R O N T J K S R V R
      T P A Q U I T A P B P H S T S D O E
      N I J U A N I C O B E T B F E T V
        I R V B U O J O U R N E Y S I I
          S P A I N C L K I S I D R O N
            T B A B T O N O
            C F G V L W
            T C R P
```

Words to Find

Author	ELIZABETH BORTON DE TREVIÑO
Title	I, JUAN DE PAREJA
Main Character	JUANICO
Supporting Characters	MASTER, MISTRESS, BROTHER ISIDRO, PAQUITA, THE KING, LOLIS, BARTOLOME
Setting	SPAIN
Words and Topics of Interest	MADRID, ART, FREEDOM, LOYALTY, DEVOTION, SEVILLE, JOURNEY
Type of Story	HISTORICAL FICTION
Newbery Honor Book	ALEXANDER, THE BLACK CALDRON

On the back of this sheet, write why you think *I, Juan de Pareja* sounds interesting.

Name _____   Date _____

Up a Road Slowly **by Irene Hunt (1967)**   **I—46**

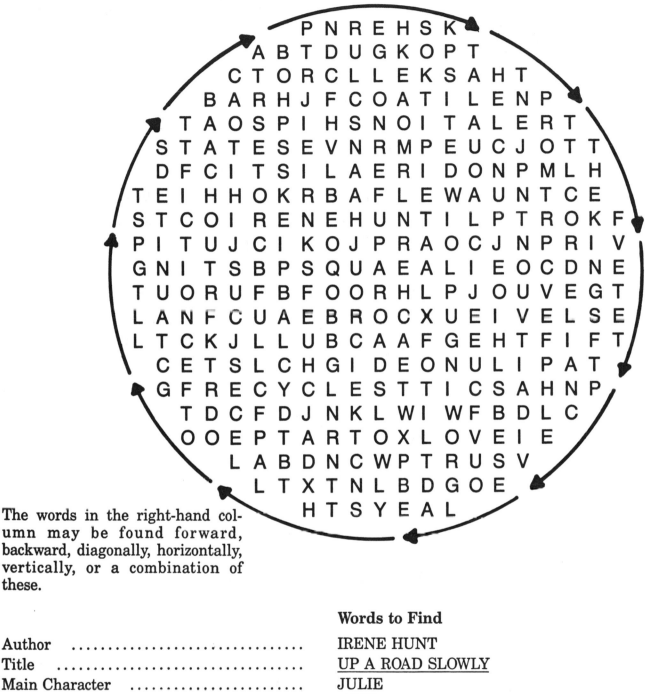

The words in the right-hand column may be found forward, backward, diagonally, horizontally, vertically, or a combination of these.

Words to Find

Author	IRENE HUNT
Title	<u>UP A ROAD SLOWLY</u>
Main Character	JULIE
Supporting Characters	LAURA, CHRIS, AUNT CORDELIA, UNCLE HASKELL
Setting	UNITED STATES
Words and Topics of Interest	DEATH, LE VIEUX CORBEAU, TEACHER, LOVE, GROWING UP, RELATIONSHIPS, FULL CYCLE
Type of Story	REALISTIC FICTION
Newbery Honor Book	O'DELL, <u>THE KING'S FIFTH</u>

On the back of this sheet, write why you think *Up a Road Slowly* sounds interesting.

**From the Mixed-Up Files of Mrs. Basil E. Frankweiler
by E. L. Konigsburg (1968)**

The words in the right-hand column may be found forward,
backward, diagonally, horizontally,
vertically, or a combination of
these.

```
              A N G E L G
            J B D G I K I   N
          O S N Y D E R   R S T
          P R S T A B N D   H J K X
        F R O M T H E M I X E D U P F
        E F N E W Y O R K C I T Y J M I
      L Q R S T U V Z A B D C D E F G L
      H T H E E G Y P T G A M E D M N E
      G R E E N W I C H I E J K E L T O
      K L N P A C B F R H L S V T W B F
        M P Q J M I C H E L A N G E L O M
        E L K O N I G S B U R G B C M D R
        T F B D C F S K L P Q A C T R E S
        R E L I E W K N A R F E L I S A B
          O B D K F Q R S T S R U X V B G K
          P U V W X Y N O I T C I F E A H L
          O C D N E W Y O R K T I M E S I M
          L P R A H M N P C R Q P O N I J
            I A R E L I E W K N A R F E L
            T B E K I J L N O R T L I
            A C F G H K M O A R C M
            N D C L A U D I A B A
            M U S E U M O F L J
```

Words to Find

Author	E. L. KONIGSBURG
Title	FROM THE MIXED-UP FILES OF MRS. BASIL E. FRANKWEILER
Main Character	CLAUDIA
Supporting Characters	JAMIE, MRS. BASIL E. FRANKWEILER
Setting	NEW YORK CITY
Words and Topics of Interest	METROPOLITAN MUSEUM OF ART, MICHELANGELO, ANGEL, NEW YORK TIMES, GREENWICH
Type of Story	DETECTIVE FICTION
Newbery Honor Book . . . . : . .	SNYDER, THE EGYPT GAME

On the back of this sheet, write why you think *From the Mixed-Up Files of Mrs. Basil E. Frankweiler* sounds interesting.

Name _____   Date _____

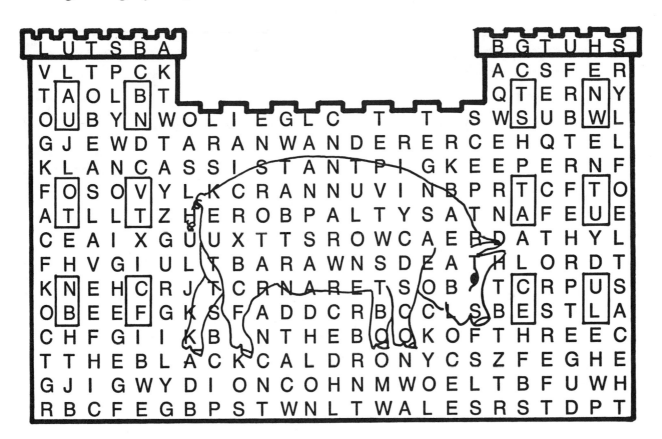

L U T S B A   B G T U H S
V L T P C K   A C S F E R
T A O L B T   Q T E R N Y
O U B Y N W O L I E G L C   T   T   S W S U B W L
G J E W D T A R A N W A N D E R E R C E H Q T E L
K L A N C A S S I S T A N T P I G K E E P E R N F
F O S O V Y L K C R A N N U V I N B P R T C F T O
A T L L T Z H E R O B P A L T Y S A T N A F E U E
C E A I X G U U X T T S R O W C A E B D A T H Y L
F H V G I U L T B A R A W N S D E A T H L O R D T
K N E H C R J T C P N A R E T S O B T C R P U S
O B E E F G K S F A D D C R B C C L S B E S T L A
C H F G I I K B N T H E B O O K O F T H R E E C
T T H E B L A C K C A L D R O N Y C S Z F E G H E
G J I G W Y D I O N C O H N M W O E L T B F U W H
R B C F E G B P S T W N L T W A L E S R S T D P T

The words in the right-hand column may be found forward, backward, diagonally, horizontally, vertically, or a combination of these.

Words to Find

Author .... LLOYD ALEXANDER

Title .... THE HIGH KING

Main Character .... TARAN

Supporting Characters .... GILONWY, GWYDION, ARAWNS DEATH LORD, EILOWNY, HENWEN, GURGI

Setting .... WALES

Words and Topics of Interest .... ASSISTANT PIG KEEPER, HERO, QUEST, ANNUVIN, DRNWYN, CAER DATHYL

Type of Story .... FANTASY

Newbery Honor Book .... LESTER, TO BE A SLAVE

Other Books in Series .... THE BOOK OF THREE, THE BLACK CALDRON, THE CASTLE OF LLYR, TARAN WANDERER

On the back of this sheet, write why you think *The High King* sounds interesting.

Name _____   Date _____

Sounder by William H. Armstrong (1970)

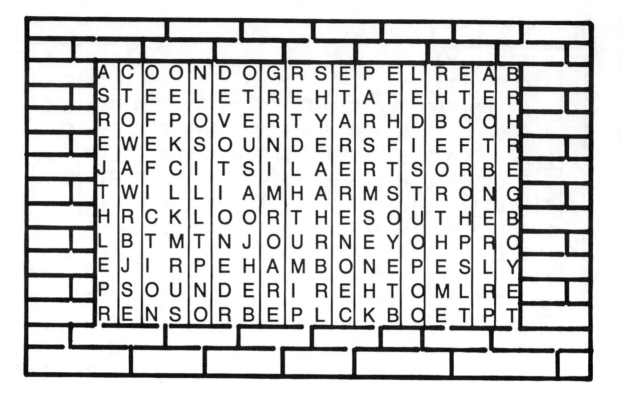

```
A C O O N D O G R S E P E L R E A B
S T E E L E T R E H T A F E H T E R
R O F P O V E R T Y A R H D B C O H
E W E K S O U N D E R S F I E F T R
J A F C I T S I L A E R T S O R B E
T W I L L I A M H A R M S T R O N G
H R C K L O O R T H E S O U T H E B
L B T M T N J O U R N E Y C H P R O
E J I R P E H A M B O N E P E S L Y
P S O U N D E R I R E H T O M L R E
R E N S O R B E P L C K B O E T P T
```

The words in the right-hand column may be found forward, backward, diagonally, horizontally, vertically, or a combination of these.

	Words to Find
Author	WILLIAM H. ARMSTRONG
Title	SOUNDER
Main Character	THE BOY
Supporting Characters	SOUNDER, THE FATHER, THE MOTHER
Setting	THE SOUTH
Words and Topics of Interest	COON DOG, POVERTY, HAM BONE, JAIL, DEVOTION
Type of Story	REALISTIC FICTION
Newbery Honor Book	STEELE, JOURNEY OUTSIDE

On the back of this sheet, write why you think *Sounder* sounds interesting.

Name _____ Date _____

Summer of the Swans by Betsy Byars (1971)

```
                          N S A R A
                        B A T B E T S Y B
                      T U W E S T V   Y
                    T   L N B D T M I   L A
              S   E R M L   B W A T C H D J R   T R
          A J U J K L N K T R E L L I W S B R T G O S
          M L O M W A N D A Q K D B S R T C H A R L   E R
          A O E M E L B Y E R H A N D I C A P P E D N T D
          R S P E T S D R N H L K N E E K N O C K R I S E
          Y T O R A N G E S O B A B B I T T L L V S A T R
          N O R E A L I S T I C F I C T I O N
          D E T H E S W A N S
```

The words in the right-hand column may be found forward, backward, diagonally, horizontally, vertically, or a combination of these.

Words to Find

Author	BETSY BYARS
Title	SUMMER OF THE SWANS
Main Character	SARA
Supporting Characters	CHARLIE, WANDA, AUNT WILLIE, MARY, JOE MELBY
Setting	WEST VIRGINIA
Words and Topics of Interest	ORANGE SNEAKERS, WATCH, LOST, HANDICAPPED, POND
Type of Story	REALISTIC FICTION
Newbery Honor Book	BABBITT, KNEEKNOCK RISE

On the back of this sheet, write why you think *Summer of the Swans* sounds interesting.

Mrs. Frisby and the Rats of NIMH by Robert C. O'Brien (1972)

```
P M R S F R I S B Y A N D T H E R A T S O F N I M H
S A H R Y E Y Z A B D I J P B C D F H J I K L T R M
V R D N P A Z W R H K C S R P T E R E S A Q W E S N
P T S J X D X P N D L O P O V L Y W Z B D F D O F P
D I H E N I S B Y R N D Q T V B C F C P J Y K L R N
T N Z R O N C F A R M E R S M A R K E T N R J X I O
X B C E F G F H R L N M T O S X Q T S F D C B S P
P R T M D J K D M P U B P W H J M P B C D B T
B P D Y F G H J K P T S C D L G R T I M O T H Y W
D F C J U S T I N U V M R A G E S B K L M
N A T I O N A L I N S T I T U T E O F M E N T A L H
F N Y Z N B F H F J K L M P B C X P D B F H X K J E
W T K X A D J K T H E H E A D L E S S C U P I D X A
X A I J T H E P L A N B D R Z H Q B D R V X P K M L
J S X D H J B C D F H M R F I T Z G I B B O N K P T
K Y N C A I B C G Z B L M P B C H K Z S I H Q R H
L M C Y N T H I A X Y W Z N E I R B O C T R E B O R
```

The words in the right-hand column may be found forward, backward, diagonally, horizontally, vertically, or a combination of these.

Words to Find

Author	ROBERT C. O'BRIEN
Title	MRS. FRISBY AND THE RATS OF NIMH
Main Character	MRS. FRISBY
Supporting Characters	JONATHAN, JEREMY, TIMOTHY, MARTIN, TERESA, CYNTHIA, MR. AGES, JUSTIN, NICODEMUS
Setting	BARNYARD
Words and Topics of Interest	FARMER'S MARKET, THE PLAN, READING, MR. FITZGIBBON, NATIONAL INSTITUTE OF MENTAL HEALTH
Type of Story	FANTASY
Newbery Honor Book	SNYDER, THE HEADLESS CUPID

On the back of this sheet, write why you think _Mrs. Frisby and the Rats of NIMH_ sounds interesting.

Name _____   Date _____

Julie of the Wolves by Jean Craighead George (1973)   **I–52**

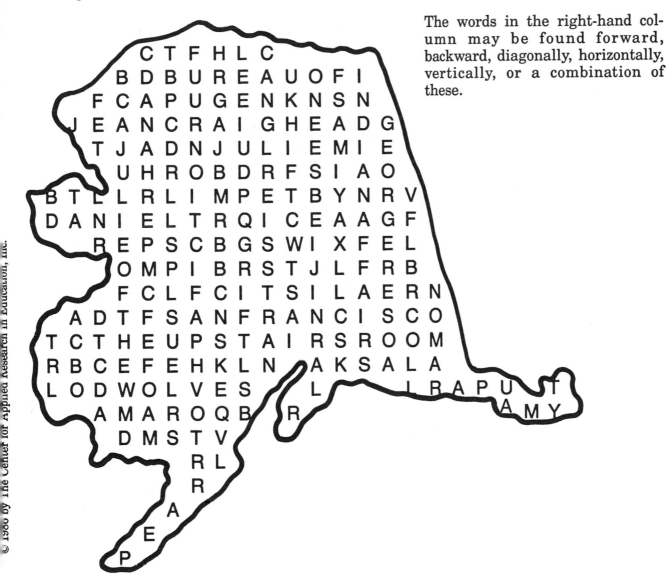

The words in the right-hand column may be found forward, backward, diagonally, horizontally, vertically, or a combination of these.

```
        C T F H L C
      B D B U R E A U O F I
      F C A P U G E N K N S N
    J E A N C R A I G H E A D G
    T J A D N J U L I E M I   E
    U H R O B D R F S I   A O
  B T L R L I M P E T B Y N R V
D A N I E L T R Q I C E A A G F
R E P S C B G S W I X F E L
O M P I B R S T J L F R B
F C L F C I T S I L A E R N
A D T F S A N F R A N C I S C O
T C T H E U P S T A I R S R O O M
R B C E F E H K L N A K S A L A
L O D W O L V E S     L   L R A P U T
    A M A R O Q B   R       A M Y
    D M S T V L
        R L
        R
        R
      A
    E
  P
```

Words to Find

Author	JEAN CRAIGHEAD GEORGE
Title	JULIE OF THE WOLVES
Main Character	JULIE MIYAX
Supporting Characters	AMAROQ, CAPUGEN, AMY, PEARL
Setting	ALASKA
Words and Topics of Interest	BUREAU OF INDIAN AFFAIRS, DANIEL, SAN FRANCISCO, RAPU
Type of Story	REALISTIC FICTION
Newbery Honor Book	REISS, THE UPSTAIRS ROOM

On the back of this sheet, write why you think *Julie of the Wolves* sounds interesting.

Name _____   Date _____

The Slave Dancer by Paula Fox (1974)

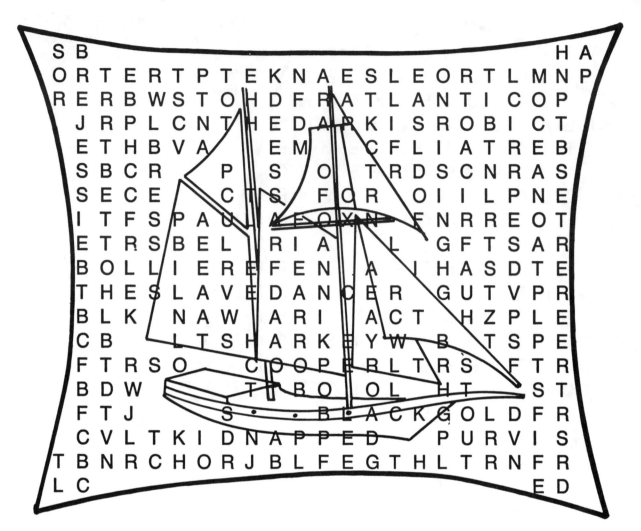

```
S B                                               H A
O R T E R T P T E K N A E S L E O R T L M N P
R E R B W S T O H D F R A T L A N T I C O P P
J R P L C N T H E D A R K I S R O B I C T
E T H B V A   E M   C F L I A T R E B
S B C R   P   S   O   T R D S C N R A S
S E C E   C T S   F O R   O I I L P N E
I T F S P A U L A F O X N   F N R R E O T
E T R S B E L   R I A   L   G F T S A R
B O L L I E R E F E N   A I H A S D T E
T H E S L A V E D A N C E R   G U T V P R
B L K   N A W   A R I   A C T   H Z P L E
C B   L T S H A R K E Y W   B   T S P E E
F T R S O   C O O P E R L T R S   F T R R
B D W   T   B O   O L   H T   S T
F T J   S . . B L A C K G O L D F R
C V L T K I D N A P P E D   P U R V I S
T B N R C H O R J B L F E G T H L T R N F R
L C                                           E D
```

The words in the right-hand column may be found forward, backward, diagonally, horizontally, vertically, or a combination of these.

Words to Find

Author	PAULA FOX
Title	<u>THE SLAVE DANCER</u>
Main Character	JESSIE BOLLIER
Supporting Characters	CAPTAIN CAWTHORNE, PURVIS, SHARKEY, STOUT, RAS
Setting	ATLANTIC OCEAN
Words and Topics of Interest	THE MOONLIGHT, KIDNAPPED, AFRICA, BLACK GOLD, SLAVER, FIFE
Type of Story	HISTORICAL FICTION
Newbery Honor Book	COOPER, <u>THE DARK IS RISING</u>

On the back of this sheet, write why you think *The Slave Dancer* sounds interesting.

Name _____   Date _____

M. C. Higgins the Great by Virginia Hamilton (1975)

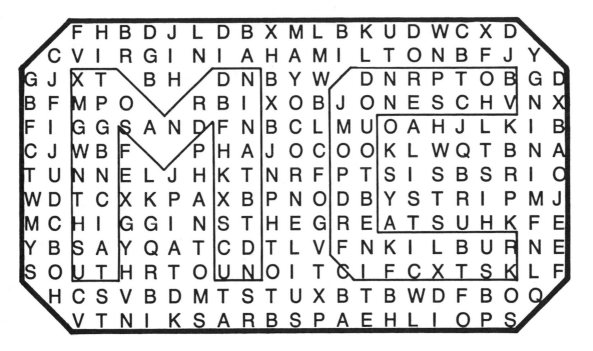

```
F H B D J L D B X M L B K U D W C X D
C V I R G I N I A H A M I L T O N B F J Y
G J X T   B H   D N B Y W   D N R P T O B G D
B F M P O   R B I X O B J O N E S C H V N X
F I G G S A N D F N B C L M U O A H J L K I B
C J W B F   P H A J O C O O K L W Q T B N A
T U N N E L J H K T N R F P T S I S B S R I O
W D T C X K P A X B P N O D B Y S T R I P M J
M C H I G G I N S T H E G R E A T S U H K F E
Y B S A Y Q A T C D T L V F N K I L B U R N E
S O U T H R T O U N O I T C I F C X T S K L F
  H C S V B D M T S T U X B T B W D F B O Q
  V T N I K S A R B S P A E H L I O P S
```

The words in the right-hand column may be found forward, backward, diagonally, horizontally, vertically, or a combination of these.

Words to Find

Author .... VIRGINIA HAMILTON

Title .... M. C. HIGGINS THE GREAT

Main Character .... MAYO CORNELIUS

Supporting Characters .... JONES, BANINA, BEN KILBURN

Setting .... SOUTH

Words and Topics of Interest .... STRIPMINING, SPOILHEAP, TUNNEL, POLE

Type of Story .... REALISTIC FICTION

Newbery Honor Book .... RASKIN, FIGGS AND PHANTOMS

On the back of this sheet, write why you think *M. C. Higgins the Great* sounds interesting.

Name _____   Date _____

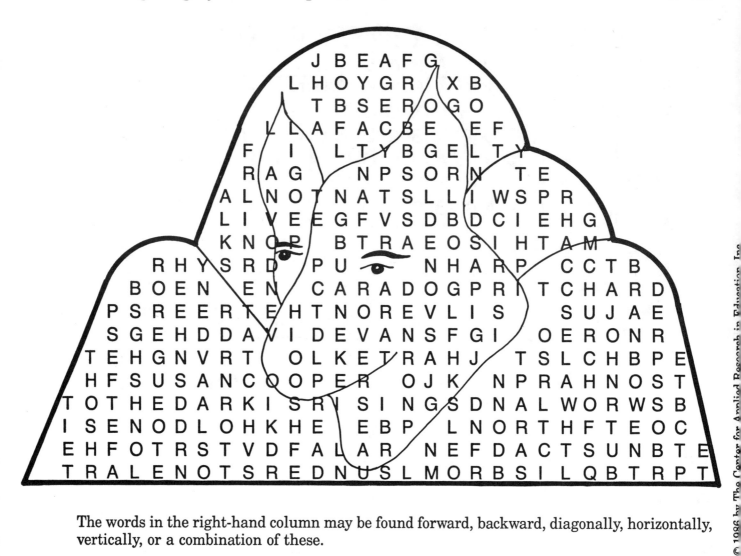

The words in the right-hand column may be found forward, backward, diagonally, horizontally, vertically, or a combination of these.

Words to Find

Author	SUSAN COOPER
Title	THE GREY KING
Main Character	WILL STANTON
Supporting Characters	DAVID EVANS, RHYS, BRAN, CAFALL, OWEN, CARA DOG PRITCHARD, JOHN ROWLANDS
Setting	NORTH WALES
Words and Topics of Interest	CHURCH OF ST. CADFEN, OLD ONES, EVIL, GOLDEN HARP, GREY FOX, QUEST
Type of Story	FANTASY
Newbery Honor Book	MATHIS, THE HUNDRED PENNY BOX
Other Books in Series	OVER SEA UNDER STONE, THE DARK IS RISING, GREENWITCH, SILVER ON THE TREE

On the back of this sheet, write why you think *The Grey King* sounds interesting.

Name _____   Date _____

Roll of Thunder, Hear My Cry by Mildred Taylor (1977)

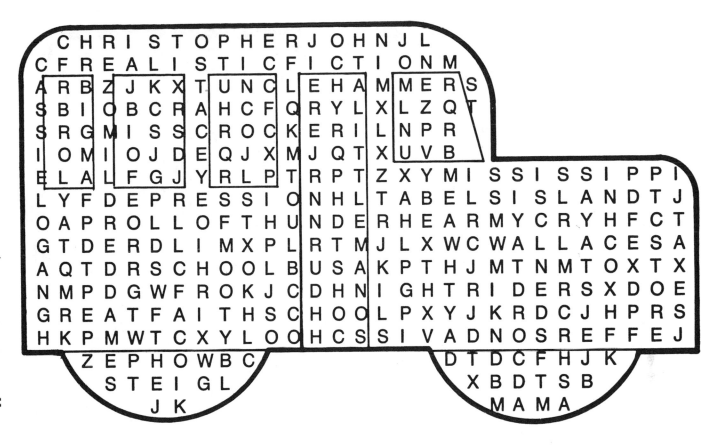

The words in the right-hand column may be found forward, backward, diagonally, horizontally, vertically, or a combination of these.

Words to Find

Author .... MILDRED TAYLOR

Title .... ROLL OF THUNDER, HEAR MY CRY

Main Character .... CASSIE LOGAN

Supporting Characters .... LITTLE MAN, STACEY, MAMA, BIG MA,
CHRISTOPHER JOHN, UNCLE
HAMMER, MISS CROCKER

Setting .... MISSISSIPPI

Words and Topics of Interest .... DEPRESSION, GREAT FAITH SCHOOL,
TAXES, JEFFERSON DAVIS SCHOOL,
NIGHT RIDERS, SCHOOL BUS,
WALLACE STORE

Type of Story .... REALISTIC FICTION

Newbery Honor Book .... STEIG, ABEL'S ISLAND

On the back of this sheet, write why you think *Roll of Thunder, Hear My Cry* sounds interesting.

Name _____   Date _____

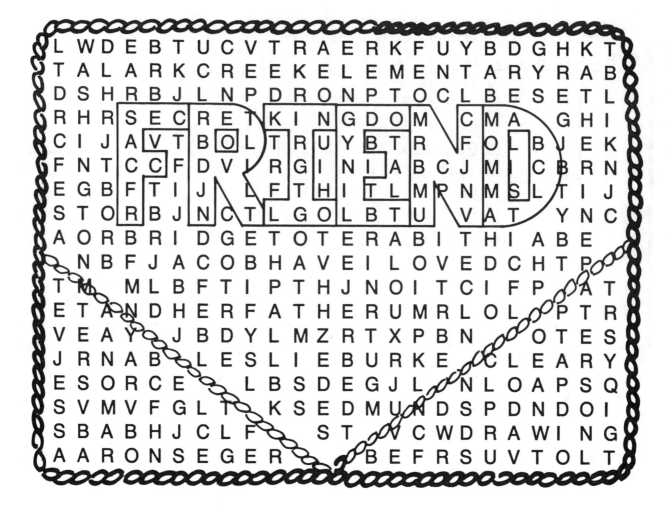

The words in the right-hand column may be found forward, backward, diagonally, horizontally, vertically, or a combination of these.

	Words to Find
Author	KATHERINE PATERSON
Title	BRIDGE TO TERABITHIA
Main Character	JESS AARONS
Supporting Characters	LESLIE BURKE, DAD, MOMMA, MAYBELLE
Setting	VIRGINIA
Words and Topics of Interest	LARK CREEK ELEMENTARY, RACING, MISS EDMUNDS, DRAWING, WASHINGTON, SECRET KINGDOM
Type of Story	REALISTIC FICTION
Newbery Honor Book	CLEARY, RAMONA AND HER FATHER
Second Newbery	JACOB HAVE I LOVED

On the back of this sheet, write why you think *Bridge to Terabithia* sounds interesting.

The Westing Game by Ellen Raskin (1979)   **I–58**

```
      S C        F J B   T
   F A F H C L U E S B D T
   G N R B O M B E R C R E
     D B R A L P E H M J O
   Y P Y A L E G N A B S V A
   V     B P D     G R A C E T
I O O O   H K M T N G O S M O K E     S G B I O O O
B T L Q     T W I N D K L O P P E L V A X Y P B P C
F D G H       I   O P A N C   F     M G   A J U P
F E V I T C E T E D   V R E R E L X E W E L T R U T
I B D C E T S S Q       Y S B T   L E N P E T B C
C T F B C E L L E N R A S K I N   T S F C R O W B
T S R A W D F T S R B N P   S R E W O T T E S N U S
I C B E T H K N D C F E L     B R U I S R O Q L C
O T H E G R E A T G I L L Y H O P K I N S C N P D R
N T S B T C A U L T C H E N F R I S B G T S V C W X
I O O O Y B P D W I S C O N S I N C J L K P I O O O
```

The words in the right-hand column may be found forward, backward, diagonally, horizontally, vertically, or a combination of these.

Words to Find

Author .... ELLEN RASKIN

Title .... THE WESTING GAME

Main Character .... TURTLE WEXLER

Supporting Characters .... SAM WESTING, ANGELA, FLORA, CROW, SANDY, GRACE

Setting .... WISCONSIN

Words and Topics of Interest .... SUNSET TOWERS, CLUES, MONEY, BOMBER, DEBTS, WINDKLOPPEL, SMOKE

Type of Story .... DETECTIVE FICTION

Newbery Honor Book .... PATERSON, THE GREAT GILLY HOPKINS

On the back of this sheet, write why you think *The Westing Game* sounds interesting.

A Gathering of Days by Joan Blos (1980)

```
D J                                           K B
B I P K M N S           T R B J L C G
D F A T H E R U L C A S S I E S H I P M A N
C D T R T L T E H R U L B K S A O K N A T R
F V B V Y N B K U C R T L D A N I E L O H P
T C V X M R S T E P M O T H E R T R P H E J
G D Z B A K B Y V L Z B N P B D L D B R R T
K N E M O H M O R F D A O R E H T L V A I Z
F P B A J E L P T E A O N E W E N G L A N D
A T E R I R S D E G N T D E U L H K N Y E B
R B K Y B D B R J R C B G F K P Q T C L C T
M L P M J I K N E W H A M P S H I R E A A V
P T R A L A G B D P J K R J A Q R B C N B A
R H J R V N K A F L N D L P J O A N B L O S
A G A T H E R I N G O F D A Y S I R S B T R
Q K B H W B S R C T L S R T E B J N B R H O
T M T A N N H I G H A M B K T S M P T R A V
V R H C B T                 J B C K L T
C T                                   L R
```

The words in the right-hand column may be found forward, backward, diagonally, horizontally, vertically, or a combination of these.

Words to Find

Author	JOAN BLOS
Title	A GATHERING OF DAYS
Main Character	CATHERINE CABOT HALL
Supporting Characters	FATHER, MARY MARTHA, CASSIE SHIPMAN
Setting	NEW HAMPSHIRE
Words and Topics of Interest	NEW ENGLAND, ANN HIGHAM, DANIEL, STEPMOTHER
Type of Story	DIARY
Newbery Honor Book	KHERDIAN, THE ROAD FROM HOME

On the back of this sheet, write why you think *A Gathering of Days* sounds interesting.

Name _____   Date _____

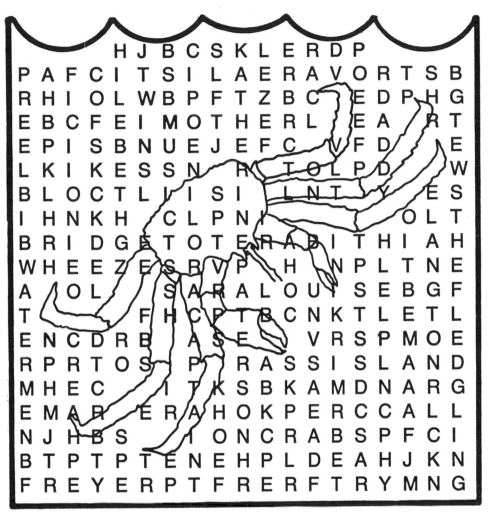

```
        H J B C S K L E R D P
    P A F C I T S I L A E R A V O R T S B
    R H I O L W B P F T Z B C E D P H G
    E B C F E I M O T H E R L E A R T
    E P I S B N U E J E F C V F D E
    L K I K E S S N R T O L P D W
    B L O C T L I S I L N T Y E S
    I H N K H C L P N I O L T
    B R I D G E T O T E R A B I T H I A H
    W H E E Z E R V P H N P L T N E
    A O L S A R A L O U S E B G F
    T F H C P T B C N K T L E T L
    E N C D R B A S E V R S P M O E
    R P R T O S P R A S S I S L A N D
    M H E C I T K S B K A M D N A R G
    E M A R E R A H O K P E R C C A L L
    N J H B S I O N C R A B S P F C I
    B T P T P T E N E H P L D E A H J K N
    F R E Y E R P T F R E R F T R Y M N G
```

The words in the right-hand column may be found forward, backward, diagonally, horizontally, vertically, or a combination of these.

Words to Find

Author	KATHERINE PATERSON
Title	JACOB HAVE I LOVED
Main Character	SARA LOUISE
Supporting Characters	CAROLINE, MOTHER, DADDY, GRANDMA, CAPTAIN, CALL
Setting	CHESAPEAKE BAY
Words and Topics of Interest	TWINS, RASS ISLAND, WATERMEN, CRABS, SPIES, WHEEZE, MUSIC, BIBLE
Type of Story	REALISTIC FICTION
Newbery Honor Book	LANGTON, THE FLEDGLING
Second Newbery	BRIDGE TO TERABITHIA

On the back of this sheet, write why you think *Jacob Have I Loved* sounds interesting.

Name _____   Date _____

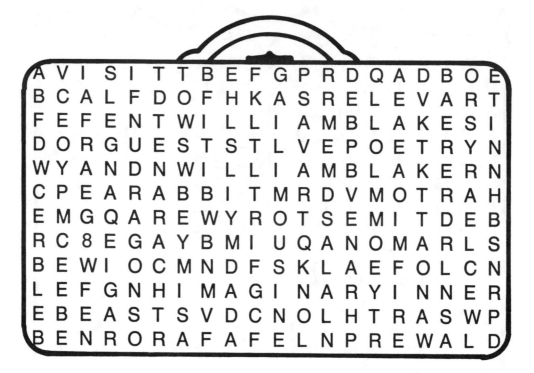

```
A V I S I T T B E F G P R D Q A D B O E
B C A L F D O F H K A S R E L E V A R T
F E F E N T W I L L I A M B L A K E S I
D O R G U E S T S T L V E P O E T R Y N
W Y A N D N W I L L I A M B L A K E R N
C P E A R A B B I T M R D V M O T R A H
E M G Q A R E W Y R O T S E M I T D E B
R C 8 E G A Y B M I U Q A N O M A R L S
B E W I O C M N D F S K L A E F O L C N
L E F G N H I M A G I N A R Y I N N E R
E B E A S T S V D C N O L H T R A S W P
B E N R O R A F A F E L N P R E W A L D
```

The words in the right-hand column may be found forward, backward, diagonally, horizontally, vertically, or a combination of these.

Author   ....

Words to Find

NANCY WILLARD

Title   ....

A VISIT TO WILLIAM BLAKE'S INN

Main Character   ....

WILLIAM BLAKE

Supporting Characters   ....

DRAGONS, ANGELS, RABBIT

Setting   ....

IMAGINARY INN

Words and Topics of Interest   ....

GUESTS, LIMOUSINE, BEASTS, MENU, BEDTIME STORY, TRAVELERS

Type of Story   ....

POETRY

Newbery Honor Book   ....

CLEARY, RAMONA QUIMBY, AGE 8

On the back of this sheet, write why you think *A Visit to William Blake's Inn* sounds interesting.

Dicey's Song by Cynthia Voigt (1983)

The words in the right-hand column may be found forward, backward, diagonally, horizontally, vertically, or a combination of these.

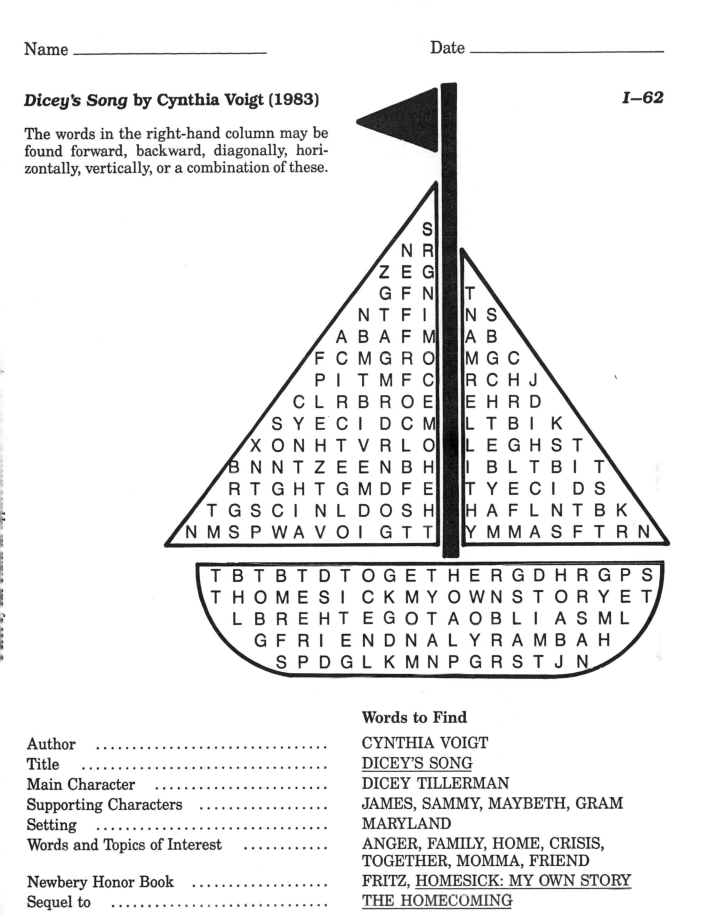

Words to Find

Author .... CYNTHIA VOIGT

Title .... DICEY'S SONG

Main Character .... DICEY TILLERMAN

Supporting Characters .... JAMES, SAMMY, MAYBETH, GRAM

Setting .... MARYLAND

Words and Topics of Interest .... ANGER, FAMILY, HOME, CRISIS, TOGETHER, MOMMA, FRIEND

Newbery Honor Book .... FRITZ, HOMESICK: MY OWN STORY

Sequel to .... THE HOMECOMING

On the back of this sheet, write why you think *Dicey's Song* sounds interesting.

Name _____   Date _____

Dear Mr. Henshaw by Beverly Cleary (1984)   I—63

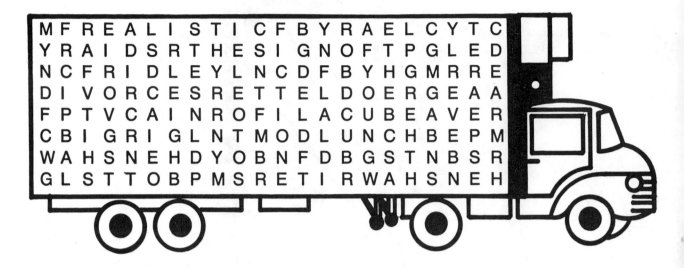

```
M F R E A L I S T I C F B Y R A E L C Y T C
Y R A I D S R T H E S I G N O F T P G L E D
N C F R I D L E Y L N C D F B Y H G M R R E
D I V O R C E S R E T T E L D O E R G E A A
F P T V C A I N R O F I L A C U B E A V E R
C B I G R I G L N T M O D L U N C H B E P M
W A H S N E H D Y O B N F D B G S T N B S R
G L S T T O B P M S R E T I R W A H S N E H
```

The words in the right-hand column may be found forward, backward, diagonally, horizontally, vertically, or a combination of these.

Words to Find

Author .... BEVERLY CLEARY

Title .... DEAR MR. HENSHAW

Main Character .... LEIGH BOTTS

Supporting Characters .... BOYD HENSHAW, MOM, DAD, MR. FRIDLEY

Setting .... CALIFORNIA

Words and Topics of Interest .... LETTERS, DIARY, DIVORCE, LUNCH BAG, BIG RIG, YOUNG WRITERS

Type of Story .... REALISTIC FICTION

Newbery Honor Book .... SPEARE, SIGN OF THE BEAVER

On the back of this sheet, write why you think *Dear Mr. Henshaw* sounds interesting.

The Hero and the Crown by Robin McKinley (1985)   **I—64**

The letters arranged within the dragon shape:

```
                                        M
                                      F
                                    S
                                    T
                              J   T E   L
                            T   G   K   H
                            E   H T U   L
                              P B C N R T   C E J
                            L T F D U G W C   L B T
                          B F A N T A S Y H K L   T A L A T
                          D J N I P M N M N I B O R   W U D
                          G S R N W O R C E H T D N A V   L C E
                          D E D S G A C K D W F K B O D R O W S
                          A N N A L A G I G O N T U R A N O U B
                          N O R T H E R N E R S   M E H D R T
                          D M H T E B L R A C L   S H T K C F
                          T A       P E     D G P E A F   N P
                            M           Y       L H       T S
                              A
                              R B
                          E M D N A E K A J E K I L
```

The words in the right-hand column may be found forward, backward, diagonally, horizontally, vertically, or a combination of these.

Words to Find

Author	ROBIN MCKINLEY
Title	THE HERO AND THE CROWN
Main Character	AERIN
Supporting Characters	ARLBETH, GALANNA, TOR, TALAT, LUTHE, AGSDED, MAUR
Setting	DAMAR
Words and Topics of Interest	SURKA, DRAGONS, GONTURAN, NORTHERNERS
Newbery Honor Book	JUKES, LIKE JAKE AND ME
Prequel	THE BLUE SWORD

On the back of this sheet, write why you think *The Hero and the Sword* sounds interesting.

Sarah, Plain and Tall by Patricia MacLachlan (1986)   **I—65**

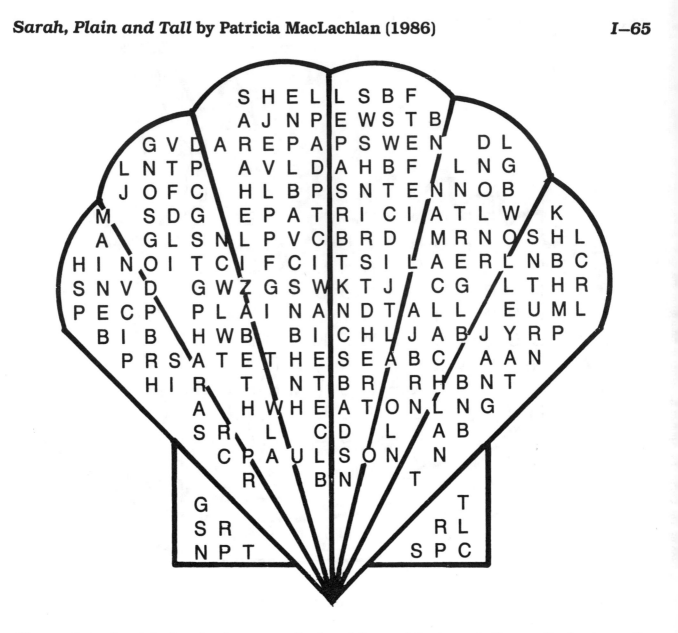

The words in the right-hand column may be found forward, backward, diagonally, horizontally, vertically, or a combination of these.

Words to Find

Author	PATRICIA MACLACHLAN
Title	SARAH, PLAIN AND TALL
Main Character	SARAH ELIZABETH WHEATON
Supporting Characters	PAPA, ANNA, CALEB
Setting	PRAIRIE
Words and Topics of Interest	SINGING, NEWSPAPER AD, MAINE, THE SEA, SEAL, YELLOW BONNET, SHELLS, AYUH, LOVE
Type of Story	REALISTIC FICTION
Newbery Honor Book	PAULSON, DOGSONG

On the back of this sheet, write why you think *Sarah, Plain and Tall* sounds interesting.

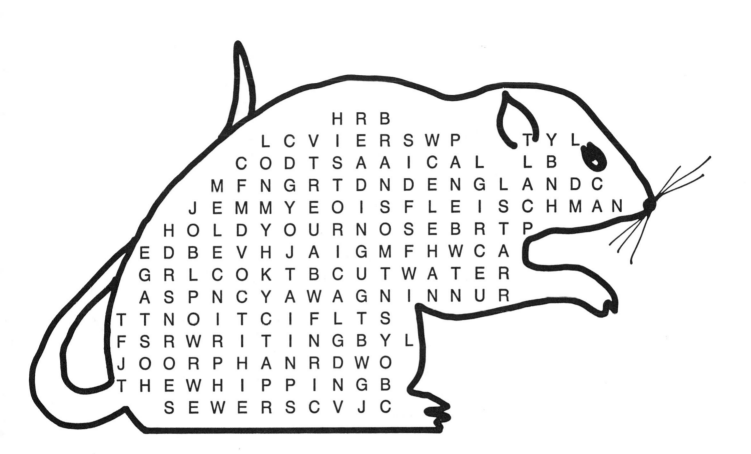

The words in the right-hand column may be found forward, backward, diagonally, horizontally, vertically, or a combination of these.

Words to Find

Author	SID FLEISCHMAN
Title	THE WHIPPING BOY
Main Character	JEMMY
Supporting Characters	PRINCE BRAT, HOLD-YOUR-NOSE-BILLY, CUTWATER
Setting	ENGLAND
Words and Topics of Interest	ORPHAN, RUNNING AWAY, RATS, HOSTAGE, SEWERS, RANSOM, READING, WRITING, GAW
Type of Story	HISTORICAL FICTION
Newbery Honor Book	BAUER, ON MY HONOR

On the back of this sheet, write why you think *The Whipping Boy* sounds interesting.

Name _____ Date _____

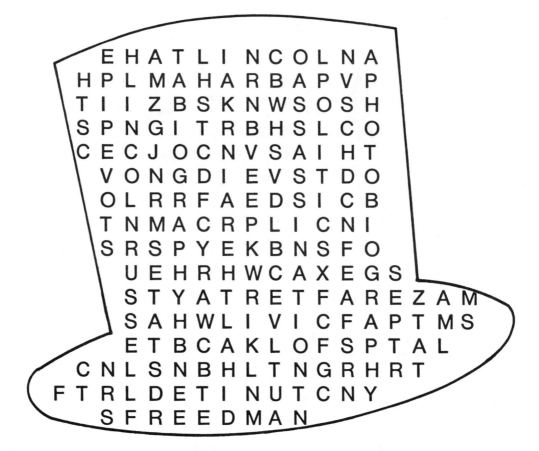

```
E H A T L I N C O L N A
H P L M A H A R B A P V P
T I I Z B S K N W S O S H
S P N G I T R B H S L C O
C E C J O C N V S A I H T
V O N G D I E V S T D O
O L R R F A E D S I C B
T N M A C R P L I C N I
S R S P Y E K B N S F O
  U E H R H W C A X E G S
  S T Y A T R E T F A R E Z A M
  S A H W L I V I C F A P T M S
  E T B C A K L O F S P T A L
C N L S N B H L T N G R H R T
F T R L D E T I N U T C N Y
  S F R E E D M A N
```

The words in the right-hand column may be found forward, backward, diagonally, horizontally, vertically, or a combination of these.

Words to Find

Author .... RUSSELL FREEDMAN

Title .... LINCOLN: A PHOTOBIOGRAPHY

Main Character .... ABRAHAM LINCOLN

Supporting Characters .... MARY

Setting .... UNITED STATES

Words and Topics of Interest .... STOVEPIPE HAT, POLITICS, PRESIDENT, CIVIL WAR, SLAVERY, LAWYER, ASSASSINATION

Type of Story .... BIOGRAPHY

Newbery Honor Book .... MAZER, AFTER THE RAIN

On the back of this sheet, write why you think *Lincoln: A Photobiography* sounds interesting.

Name _____ Date _____

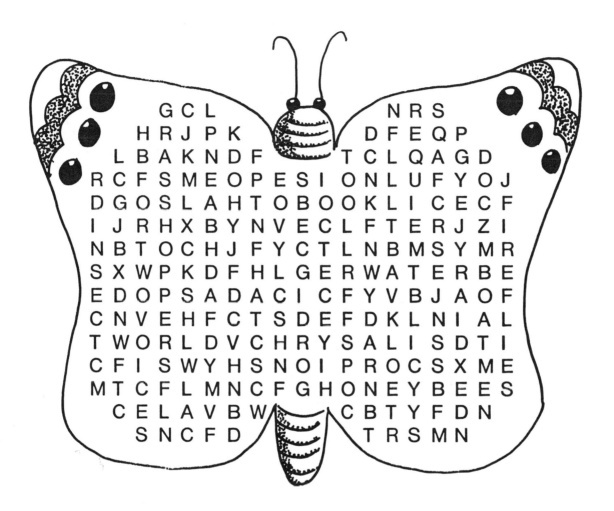

```
          G C L                            N R S
        H R J P K                        D F E Q P
      L B A K N D F            T C L Q A G D
    R C F S M E O P E S I   O N L U F Y O J
    D G O S L A H T O B O O K L I  C E C F
    I J R H X B Y N V E C L F T E R J Z I
    N B T O C H J F Y C T L N B M S Y M R
    S X W P K D F H L G E R W A T E R B E
    E D O P S A D A C I  C F Y V B J A O F
    C N V E H F C T S D E F D K L N I  A L
    T W O R L D V C H R Y S A L I  S D T I
    C F I S W Y H S N O I  P R O C S X M E
    M T C F L M N C F G H O N E Y B E E S
      C E L A V B W    C B T Y F D N
        S N C F D        T R S M N
```

The words in the right-hand column may be found forward, backward, diagonally, horizontally, vertically or a combination of these.

Words to Find

Author . . . .   PAUL FLEISCHMAN

Title . . . .   JOYFUL NOISE: POEMS FOR TWO
                                        VOICES

Setting . . . .   INSECT WORLD

Words and Topics of Interest   . . . .   WATER BOATMEN, GRASSHOPPERS,
                                          FIREFLIES, CICADAS, BOOK LICE,
                                          HONEYBEES, REQUIEM,
                                          CHRYSALIS DIARY, MAYFLIES

Type of Story . . . .   POETRY

Newbery Honor Book   . . . .   MYERS, SCORPIONS

On the back of this sheet, write why you think *Joyful Noise: Poems for Two Voices* sounds interesting.

Number the Stars by Lois Lowry (1990)   **I–69**

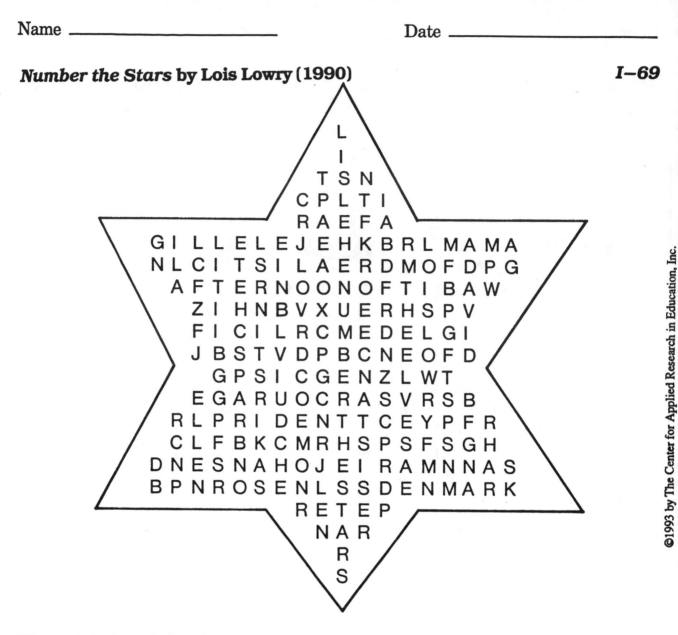

The words in the right-hand column may be found forward, backward, diagonally, horizontally, vertically, or a combination of these.

Words to Find

Author   . . . .   LOIS LOWRY

Title   . . . .   NUMBER THE STARS

Main Character   . . . .   ANNMARIE JOHANSEN

Supporting Characters   . . . .   ELLEN ROSEN, MAMA, PAPA, KIRSTI, PETER

Setting   . . . .   DENMARK

Words and Topics of Interest   . . . .   NAZIS, RESISTANCE, SWEDEN, COURAGE, FEAR, PRIDE, STAR OF DAVID, GILLELEJE

Type of Story   . . . .   REALISTIC FICTION

Newbery Honor Book   . . . .   LISLE, AFTERNOON OF THE ELVES

On the back of this sheet, write why you think _Number the Stars_ sounds interesting.

Name _____   Date _____

Maniac Magee by Jerry Spinelli (1991)   *I–70*

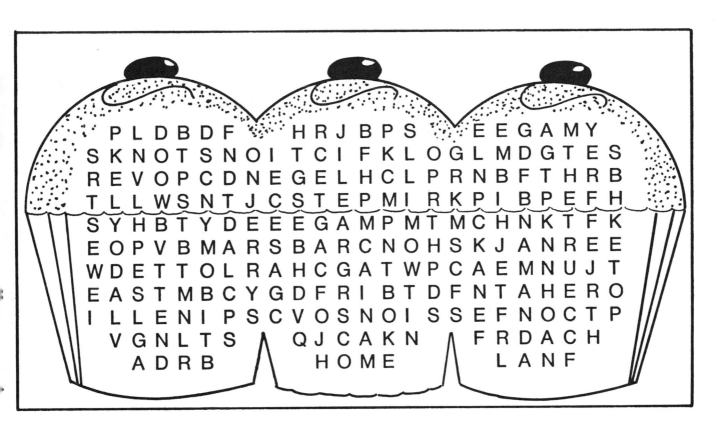

```
P L D B D F    H R J B P S    E E G A M Y
S K N O T S N O I T C I F K L O G L M D G T E S
R E V O P C D N E G E L H C L P R N B F T H R B
T L L W S N T J C S T E P M I R K P I B P E F H
S Y H B T Y D E E E G A M P M T M C H N K T F K
E O P V B M A R S B A R C N O H S K J A N R E E
W D E T T O L R A H C G A T W P C A E M N U J T
E A S T M B C Y G D F R I B T D F N T A H E R O
I L L E N I P S C V O S N O I S S E F N O C T P
V G N L T S    Q J C A K N    F R D A C H
A D R B        H O M E        L A N F
```

The words in the right-hand column may be found forward, backward, diagonally, horizontally, vertically, or a combination of these.

Words to Find

Author	JERRY SPINELLI
Title	MANIAC MAGEE
Main Character	JEFFREY MAGEE
Supporting Characters	AMANDA, GRAYSON, MARS BAR
Setting	TWO MILLS
Words and Topics of Interest	ORPHAN, RUNNING, SNEAKERS, EAST END, WEST END, KRIMPETS, COBBLE'S KNOT, HERO, HOME
Type of Story	FANTASTIC FICTION
Newbery Honor Book	AVI, THE TRUE CONFESSIONS OF CHARLOTTE DOYLE

On the back of this sheet, write why you think *Maniac Magee* sounds interesting.

Shiloh by Phyllis Reynolds Naylor (1992)   *I–71*

```
C P B J V I R G I N I A H
T H D E R T G K O M S V L
P Y T R A M S I S H W C
R L C B E G T E I T D N
C E L H T F C L L W U S K
T S I W N I K O E L R E
M T S G F R H B X C T C
S O R C I T S I L A E R
L N E G K S L I E S H E
D O G Y F D R L R M J T T
A V I N O T H I N B U T
R E B O N L S H R N D B
M A I L R O U T L E C D Z
D A D T D S R E V A R T F
F G L N S N A Y L O R N C
```

The words in the right-hand column may be found forward, backward, diagonally, horizontally, vertically, or a combination of these.

Words to Find

Author .... PHYLLIS REYNOLDS NAYLOR

Title .... SHILOH

Main Character .... MARTY PRESTON

Supporting Characters .... DAD, MA, JUDD TRAVERS, DOG

Setting .... WEST VIRGINIA

Words and Topics of Interest .... FEAR, LOVE, LIES, MAIL ROUTE, HILLS, SECRET, BEAGLE

Type of Story .... REALISTIC FICTION

Newbery Honor Book .... AVI, NOTHING BUT THE TRUTH

On the back of this sheet, write why you think *Shiloh* sounds interesting.

Name ————————————   Date ————————————

Missing May by Cynthia Rylant (1993)

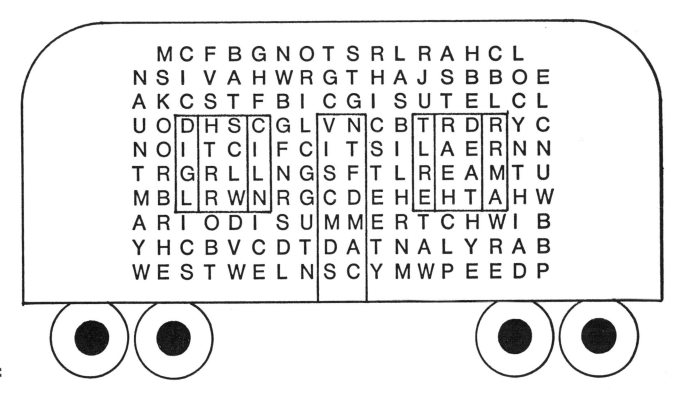

The words in the right-hand column may be found forward, backward, diagonally, horizontally, vertically, or a combination of these.

Words to Find

Author	CYNTHIA RYLANT
Title	MISSING MAY
Main Character	SUMMER
Supporting Characters	AUNT MAY, UNCLE OB, CLETUS
Setting	WEST VIRGINIA
Words and Topics of Interest	DEATH, LIFE, LOVE, WHIRLIGIGS, BATS, DEEP WATER, CHARLESTON, OWL
Type of Story	REALISTIC FICTION
Newbery Honor Book	BROOKS, WHAT HEARTS

On the back of this sheet, write why you think *Missing May* sounds interesting.

THE CALDECOTT AWARD

section II

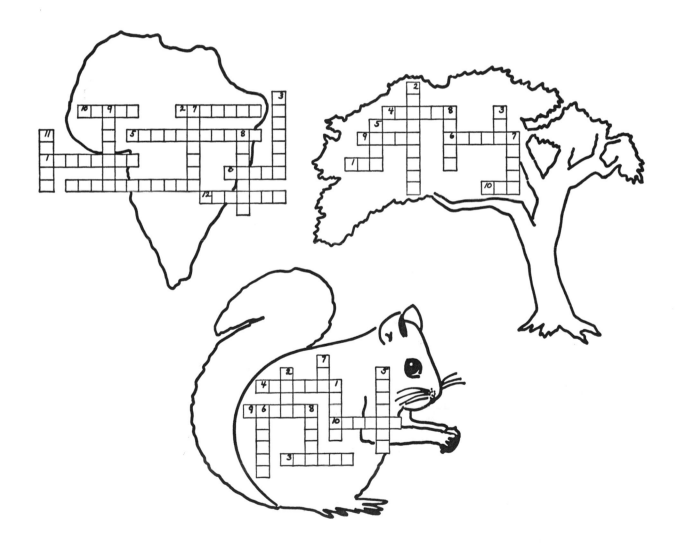

A BRIEF HISTORY OF THE CALDECOTT AWARD

In 1937, Frederic Melcher again addressed the American Library Association and proposed that a second award be established. He contended that picture books should not compete for the Newbery Award, but should be recognized in their own right. This award would be given to the illustrator and be named in honor of Randolph Caldecott, a 19th century illustrator of picture books.

The proposal was accepted, and the Caldecott Award, which was to be given to the artist of "the most distinguished American picture book for children published in the United States during the preceding year," took its rightful place beside the Newbery Award.

Rene Chambellan was again commissioned to design a medal, which was struck in bronze, and Frederic Melcher accepted the responsibility to have the medal struck each year. Since Melcher's death in 1963, his family has continued the tradition.

The winner of the Caldecott Award, selected by a committee of the American Library Association, is announced at the midwinter meeting of the American Library Association.

HOW TO USE THIS SECTION

The Caldecott Award winners provide a collection that is available in every school and public library, so each of the following puzzles can be used by your students. Although the award is given to the illustrator, the text is of equal excellence.

The clues given in these crossword puzzles are developed in the sequential order of the books' events. They provide a review and reinforcement of the story and set the order of events firmly in the students' minds. With some practice, students should then begin to pay closer attention to events and details occurring in the book to enable them to complete the puzzle without having to refer back to the book. Their skills in the areas of sequencing and recall also will be sharpened, which will increase their sense of achievement and enable them to transfer these skills to other areas of the curriculum where increased awareness of detail is needed.

To help you introduce the books to students, this section features:

- "The Caldecott Award Winners," a list that can be copied for each student to use as a checklist for choosing a title, locating the book on the shelf, and checking off the title when read.
- 56 crossword puzzles based on the Caldecott Award titles. These puzzles may be used:
  ...with a whole class following the reading of the book by the librarian or classroom teacher. Make a transparency of the puzzle and complete it together using the overhead projector *or* give each student a copy of the puzzle to complete independently or in small groups.
  ...by individual students who select a book from the collection and complete the puzzle after the story is read. A folder can be kept by each student and checked by the librarian or classroom teacher. The puzzle can serve as a basis for an oral book report or discussion between student and librarian or student and classroom teacher. The student can work on his or her own puzzle independently with the librarian or classroom teacher checking at intervals. The students can color the puzzle design after completing the puzzle.

THE CALDECOTT AWARD WINNERS

Check
Books
Read

1938: Fish (Lathrop), *Animals of the Bible*

1939: Handfoth, *Mei Li*

1940: d'Aulaire, *Abraham Lincoln*

1941: Lawson, *They Were Strong and Good*

1942: McCloskey, *Make Way for Ducklings*

1943: Burton, *The Little House*

1944: Thurber (Slobodkin), *Many Moons*

1945: Field (Jones), *Prayer for a Child*

1946: Petersham, *The Rooster Crows*

1947: MacDonald (Weisgard), *The Little Island*

1948: Tresselt (Duvoisin), *White Snow, Bright Snow*

1949: Hader, *The Big Snow*

1950: Politi, *Song of the Swallows*

1951: Milhous, *The Egg Tree*

1952: Lipkind (Mordvinoff), *Finders Keepers*

1953: Ward, *The Biggest Bear*

THE CALDECOTT AWARD WINNERS (Continued)

**Check
Books
Read**

1954: Bemelmans, *Madeline's Rescue*

1955: Perrault (Brown), *Cinderella*

1956: Langstaff (Rojankovsky), *Frog Went A-Courtin'*

1957: Udry (Simont), *A Tree Is Nice*

1958: McCloskey, *Time of Wonder*

1959: Chaucer (Cooney), *Chanticleer and the Fox*

1960: Ets, *Nine Days to Christmas*

1961: Robbins (Sidjakov), *Baboushka and the Three Kings*

1962: Brown, *Once a Mouse...*

1963: Keats, *The Snowy Day*

1964: Sendak, *Where the Wild Things Are*

1965: De Regniers (Montresor), *May I Bring a Friend?*

1966: Sorche Nic Leodhas (Hogrogian), *Always Room for One More*

1967: Ness, *Sam, Bangs and Moonshine*

1968: Emberley, *Drummer Hoff*

1969: Ransome (Shulevitz), *The Fool of the World and the Flying Ship*

Name _____   Date _____

THE CALDECOTT AWARD WINNERS (Continued)

Check
Books
Read

1970: Steig, *Sylvester and the Magic Pebble*

1971: Haley, *A Story, A Story: An African Tale*

1972: Hogrogian, *One Fine Day*

1973: Mosel (Lent), *The Funny Little Woman*

1974: Zemach, *Duffy and the Devil*

1975: McDermott, *Arrow to the Sun*

1976: Aardema (Dillon), *Why Mosquitoes Buzz in People's Ears*

1977: Musgrove (Dillon), *Ashanti to Zulu*

1978: Spier, *Noah's Ark*

1979: Goble, *The Girl Who Loved Wild Horses*

1980: Hall (Cooney), *Ox-Cart Man*

1981: Lobel, *Fables*

1982: Van Allsburg, *Jumanji*

1983: Cendrars (Brown), *Shadow*

1984: Provensen, *The Glorious Flight*

1985: Hodges (Hyman), *Saint George and the Dragon*

Name _____   Date _____

**Check
Books
Read**

1986: Van Allsburg, *The Polar Express*

1987: Yorinks (Egielski), *Hey, Al* _____

1988: Yolan, *Owl Moon* _____

1989: Ackerman, *Song and Dance Man* _____

1990: Young, *Lon Po Po* _____

1991: Macauley, *Black and White* _____

1992: Wiesner, *Tuesday* _____

1993: McCully, *Mirette on the High Wire* _____

1994: _____

1995: _____

Name _____   Date _____

Animals of the Bible by Helen Dean Fish (1938)   *II–1*
illustrated by Dorothy Lathrop

1. _____ was told to build an ark of gopher wood.
2. They that wait upon the Lord are like the mighty _____.
3. Daniel was cast into a den of _____.
4. _____ was swallowed by a great fish.
5. The animals gathered around the Christmas _____.
6. There appeared in the sky a host of heavenly _____.

7. The prodigal son returned to ask his _____ forgiveness.
8. The woman's faith was so great that Jesus healed her _____.
9. The man that was fell upon by thieves was helped by the Good _____.
10. The Good Shepherd would lay down his life for his _____.
11. Jesus rode into town on the _____ Sunday colt.
12. Peter denied the Lord _____ times before the cock crowed.

Mei Li by Thomas Handforth (1939)

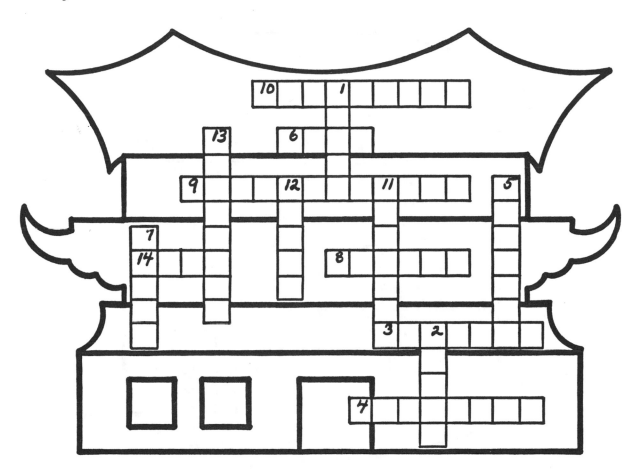

1. The setting of the story is North _____.

2. Mei Li's brother's name is _____.

3. Mci Li's mother's name is _____.

4. The family is celebrating _____ Day.

5. The _____ god is honored on this day.

6. Mei Li wants to go to the _____.

7. Mei Li brings _____ pennies to spend.

8. Mei Li gives one penny to a _____ girl.

9. Mei Li spends another penny for _____.

10. Mei Li feeds the tame _____.

11. Mei Li's fortune is to rule over a _____.

12. A _____ carries Mei Li home.

13. _____ is Mei Li's new title.

14. Mei Li's kingdom is her _____.

Name _____   Date _____

1. Abraham Lincoln was born in the state of _____.
2. Abe's nickname was "_____ Abe."
3. Abe's sister's name was _____.
4. Abe studied to be a _____.
5. Abe's best friend was _____ Speed.
6. The first war Abe fought in was the _____ War.
7. Abe's first job was that of a _____.

8. Abe's first political office was a _____ man.
9. Abe's wife's name was _____ Todd.
10. The name of one of Abe's son was _____.
11. Abe became _____ of the United States.
12. The war between the states was called the _____ War.
13. The North fought against the South and the _____ won.
14. Abe's famous speech was the _____ Address.

Name _____ Date _____

They Were Strong and Good by Robert Lawson (1941)

1. My mother's father was a _____ sea captain.
2. My mother's father's ship was the _____ Hopper.
3. My mother's mother was a little _____ girl.
4. My mother went to a _____ school.
5. My father's father was always _____ something.
6. One day, my father's father came to my father's mother's town to fight _____.

7. He met my father's mother and they were _____.
8. My father fought in the _____ War.
9. My father met my mother in _____.
10. They married and had many children. One of them was _____.
11. My father and mother and their fathers and mothers helped build our _____.
12. I am _____ of them.

Name _____   Date _____

Make Way for Ducklings by Robert McCloskey (1942)

1. Mr. and Mrs. _____ searched for a place to live.
2. They spent a night in the city of _____.
3. They found an island in the _____ Garden.
4. A bird called a _____ startled them.
5. People riding on the huge bird fed them _____.
6. They finally settled on an island in the _____ River.
7. They made friends with a policeman named _____.

8. Soon, Mrs. Mallard laid _____ eggs.
9. Mr. Mallard planned to meet Mrs. Mallard in the Public Garden in _____ week.
10. Michael held up _____ so Mrs. Mallard and the ducklings could cross the street.
11. At the Public Garden, the _____ stopped traffic.
12. After crossing the street, Mrs. Mallard and the ducklings turned to say _____.
13. The Mallards decided to live on the _____.
14. During the day, they _____ the swan boats.
15. At night, they swim to the island to _____.

Name _____   Date _____

The Little House by Virginia Lee Burton (1943)

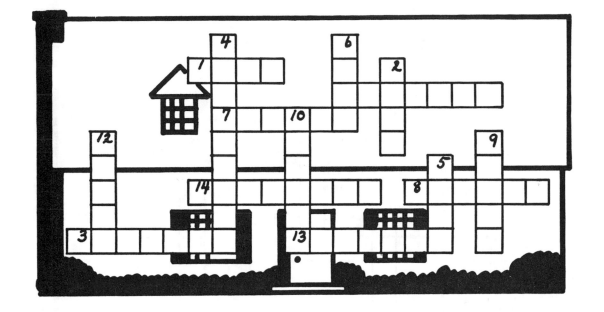

1. The man said, "This little house shall never be _____."
2. The days changed but the Little House stayed the _____.
3. She watched the _____ come and go.
4. One day the _____ carriages came.
5. A _____ was built right by the Little House.
6. Soon, the Little House was in the middle of the _____.
7. A _____ was built under the Little House.

8. The Little House was sad and _____.
9. One spring morning, the great _____ granddaughter saw the Little House.
10. They put the Little House on _____.
11. _____ was held up for hours.
12. They found a little hill with _____ trees.
13. The Little House _____ down on her new foundation.
14. All was quiet and _____ in the country again.

Name _____   Date _____

Many Moons by James Thurber (1944)
illustrated by Louis Slobodkin

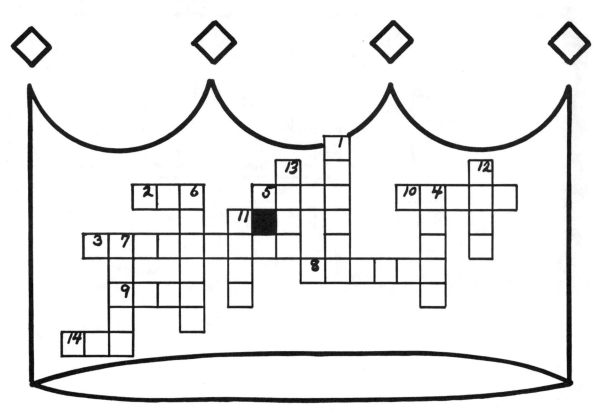

1. The little girl's name was Princess
   _____.
2. The princess was _____ years old.
3. The princess's illness was caused by too
   many _____ tarts.
4. The king told the princess, she could
   have anything her _____ desired.
5. All the princess wanted was the
   _____.
6. All the king's men said _____ can
   get the moon.
7. This made the king very _____.

8. The court _____ said he would try.
9. The princess said the moon was made of
   _____.
10. The princess received the moon on a
    golden _____.
11. The princess believed a new moon
    would _____ in its place.
12. The court jester and the moon seemed
    to _____.
13. We know the princess has only a
    _____ of the moon.
14. The real moon is still in the _____.

Name _____   Date _____

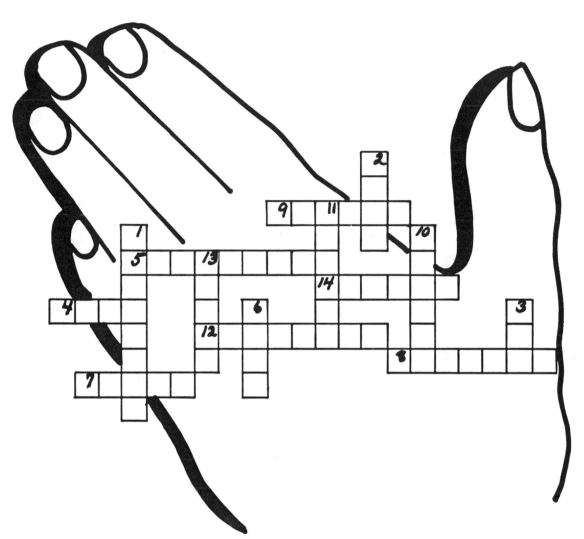

1. The child is _____ the important things in her life.
2. She blesses the _____ she drinks.
3. She blesses the _____ in which she sleeps.
4. She blesses the _____ with which she plays.
5. She blesses the _____ by which she can see at night.
6. She blesses the _____ that keeps her warm.
7. She blesses the _____ that care for her.

8. She blesses the _____ that keep her company.
9. She blesses her _____ with whom she lives.
10. She blesses her _____ because he loves her.
11. She blesses her _____ because she loves her.
12. She blesses all the _____ in the world.
13. She asks that she might sleep in _____.
14. She asks that she might wake in good _____.

Name _____   Date _____

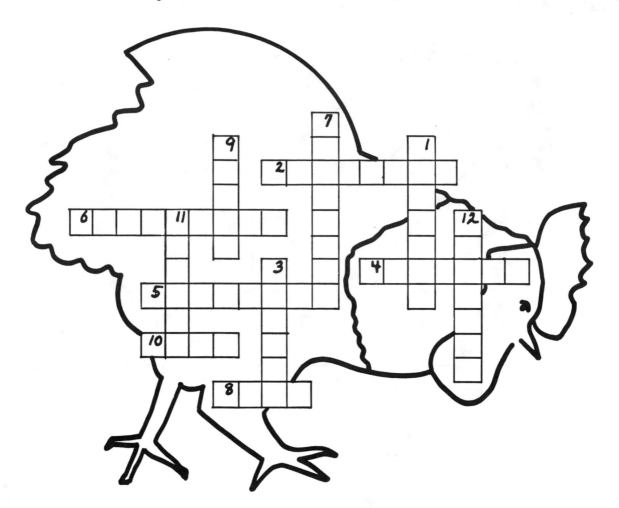

1. There are rhymes and _____ in this book.
2. One rhyme is "A Bear Went Over the _____."
3. There are _____ games in this part of the book.
4. One game is "Here's the Church, Here's the _____."
5. The next section has rope _____ rhymes.
6. One rhyme is "Teddy Bear _____."

7. The next section has _____ out games.
8. One rhyme is "_____ had a Little Lamb."
9. The next section has _____.
10. One jingle in this part is "_____ Porridge Hot."
11. The last section is titled _____.
12. In this verse, we meet _____ Washington.

Name _____   Date _____

The Little Island by Golden MacDonald (1947)
illustrated by Leonard Weisgard

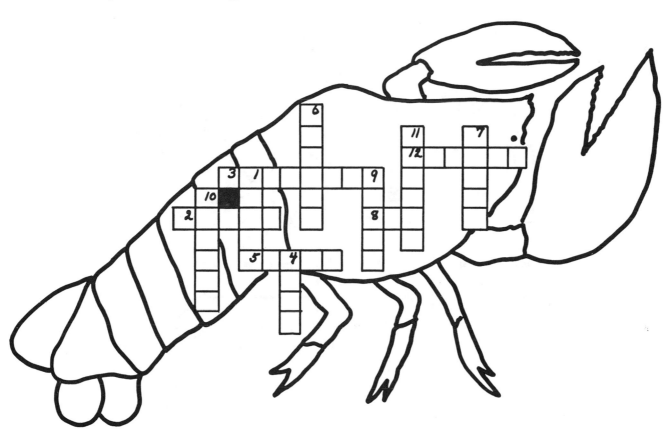

1. There is a little island in the _____.
2. Mornings are very _____ on the island.
3. _____ crawl in and hide under the rocks and ledges to shed their shells.
4. The _____ come to the island to raise their babies.
5. The birds build their _____.
6. A little black _____ comes in a boat.

7. _____ is believing about what you don't know.
8. All the land is _____ land under the sea.
9. A _____ blows in from the southeast.
10. The yellow pears drop to the ground in the _____.
11. The snow falls softly in the _____.
12. It is good to be a little _____.

White Snow, Bright Snow by Alvin Tresselt (1948)
illustrated by Roger Duvoisin

1. They all said it was going to _____.
2. The _____ waited for the first snowflake.
3. _____ hid in their warm burrows.
4. The automobiles looked like big fat _____.
5. The policeman's wife _____ a long scarf for him.
6. The children _____ in the snow.
7. The _____ began to melt the snow.
8. Pussy _____ began to bud.
9. Early spring _____ began to bud.
10. The children waited for the first _____.
11. _____ was over.
12. _____ was here.

Name _____   Date _____

The Big Snow by Berta and Elmer Hader (1949)

1. The _____ flying south was the first sign of winter.
2. The animals were getting ready for the _____ weather.
3. Some of the animals would sleep all _____.
4. The other animals were busy _____ food.
5. The rainbow around the moon meant a _____ was coming.

6. The food was gone and the animals were _____.
7. A little old _____ shoveled a path through the snow.
8. A little old _____ scattered seeds, nuts, and crumbs.
9. The ground hog woke up and saw his _____.
10. It was a long winter, but the little old man and the little old woman fed the animals until _____.

Name _____   Date _____

1. The boy's name is _____.
2. The gardener's name is _____.
3. The name of the village is _____.
4. The story takes place at the _____.
5. The birds in the story are _____.
6. The boy always carries _____ in his pocket.
7. The boy made a _____ in front of his house.

8. The birds leave at the end of _____.
9. The birds return in the _____.
10. The birds always return on _____ Day.
11. The children have a _____ on that day.
12. The _____ are rung when the birds return.
13. _____ nested in the boy's garden.
14. The boy felt a great _____ for the birds.

Name _____   Date _____

The Egg Tree by Katherine Milhous (1951)

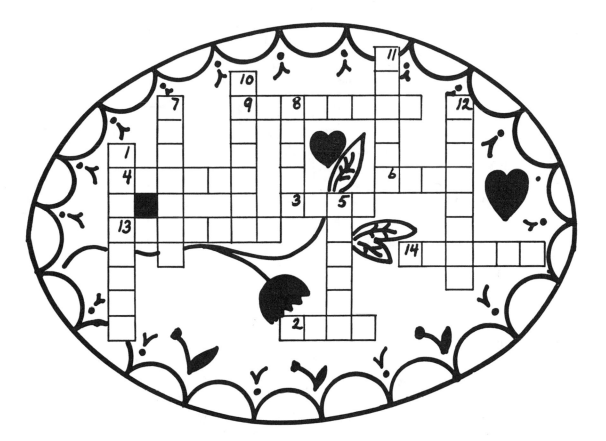

1. The story takes place at a little _____.
2. The girl's name is _____.
3. The boy's name is _____.
4. They are celebrating _____.
5. The animal they are watching for is a _____.
6. The animal will leave _____ for them to find.
7. The _____ will help them search.

8. The girl climbs to the _____ to search.
9. She finds _____'s special eggs.
10. They make an _____.
11. The next year, many _____ come to see it.
12. They bring _____.
13. There were one _____ eggs on the tree.
14. The girl scatters _____ on the lawn.

Name _____   Date _____

Finders Keepers by William Lipkind (1952)
illustrated by Nicolas Mordvinoff

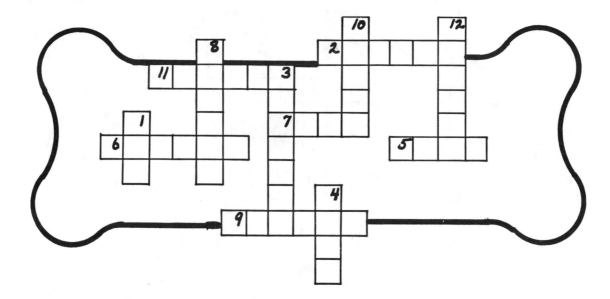

1. One dog's name is _____.
2. The other dog's name is _____.
3. They were _____ in the yard.
4. They found a _____.
5. Each dog said, "It's _____."
6. They asked a _____ to help settle the argument.

7. Then they asked a _____ to help settle the argument.
8. Then they asked a _____ to help settle the argument.
9. Then they asked a _____ to help settle the argument.
10. They had to _____ to get their bone back.
11. Finally, they settled down and _____ the bone.
12. The dogs learned a _____.

Name _____   Date _____

The Biggest Bear by Lynd Ward (1953)   *II–16*

1. Johnny _____ lived on a farm.
2. Johnny's grandfather had planted _____ trees.
3. Most barns had a _____ hung up to dry.
4. Johnny went looking for a bear and found a _____.
5. The bear grew and grew and caused all sorts of _____.
6. The bear even liked _____ for Sunday breakfast.

7. The bear's favorite food was _____.
8. Johnny had to take the bear back to the _____.
9. No matter where Johnny left him, the bear always _____.
10. Johnny thought he would have to _____ the bear.
11. Instead, Johnny and the bear ended up in a _____.
12. Johnny was happy because the men took the bear to the _____.

Madeline's Rescue by Ludwig Bemelmans (1954)

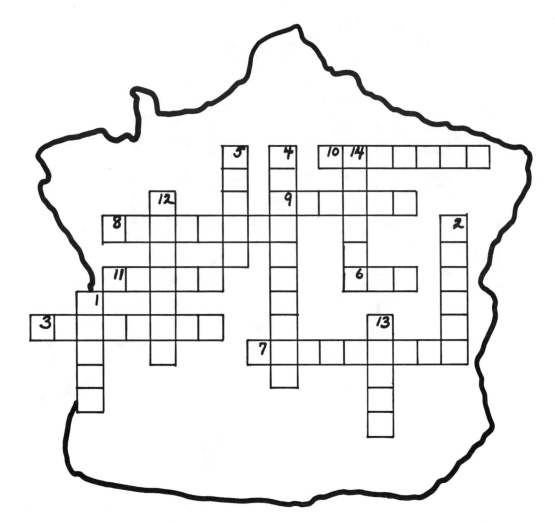

1. The setting of the story is the city of _____.
2. _____ little girls lived at a school.
3. Madeline was the _____.
4. _____ took care of them.
5. One day, Madeline fell into the _____.
6. A _____ rescued her.
7. The girls named the rescuer _____.

8. The _____ came to school for the annual inspection.
9. They said, "No dogs in _____."
10. The girls were sad. The dog _____.
11. But later the dog came back. The girls were _____.
12. Surprise! The dog had _____.
13. Now, the girls won't have to _____ over one dog.
14. There are enough dogs to go _____.

Name _____   Date _____

Cinderella translated by Marcia Brown (1955)

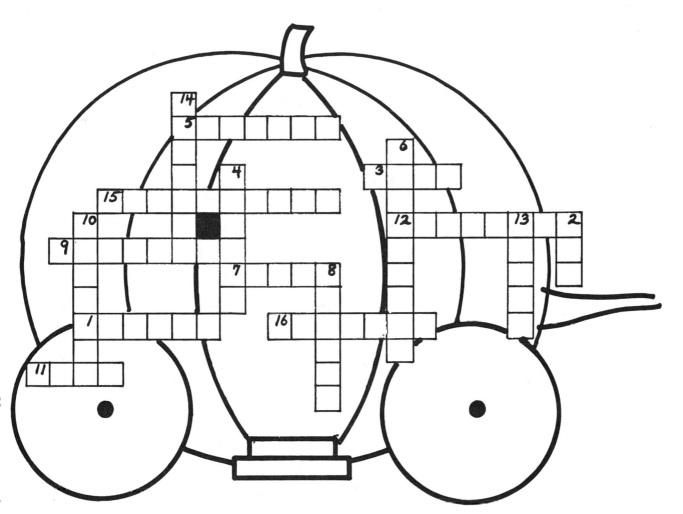

1. Cinderella had a wicked step _____.
2. The woman had _____ daughters.
3. Cinderella had to do all the _____ in the house.
4. The _____ was to give a ball.
5. Cinderella was not _____.
6. Cinderella's Fairy _____ found her in tears.
7. The pumpkin was turned into a _____.
8. The mice became a set of six _____.

9. A rat became the _____.
10. Six lizards became six _____.
11. The fairy godmother's _____ changed Cinderella's dress.
12. Cinderella had to be home by _____.
13. Cinderella lost her _____ slipper.
14. The prince had every girl in the _____ try on the slipper.
15. The slipper fit only _____'s foot.
16. The prince and Cinderella were _____.

Name _____   Date _____

Frog Went A-Courtin' by John Langstaff (1956)
illustrated by Feodor Rojankovsky

1. Frog was courting Miss _____.
2. _____ Rat agreed to the wedding.
3. Old Miss _____ made the wedding gown.
4. The little white _____ spread the cloth.
5. The big _____ bug carried a cider jug.
6. Mr. Coon brought a _____ spoon.
7. The spotted _____ passed the wedding cake.
8. The bumblebee had a _____ on his knee.
9. The nimble _____ danced a jig.
10. The old gray _____ cut loose.
11. _____ little ants were fixing to have a dance.
12. The little old fly ate up the _____ pie.
13. The little chick ate too much and got _____.
14. The old tomcat _____ everything.
15. Frog and Mouse went to _____.

Name _____   Date _____

A Tree Is Nice by Janice May Udry (1957)
illustrated by Marc Simont

1. Trees fill up the _____.
2. Trees make everything _____.
3. Even _____ is nice to have.
4. It is fun to play in the _____ in the fall.
5. Tree limbs make great places to _____.

6. It is fun to pick _____ from trees.
7. A tree is a good place to hang a _____.
8. Animals and people enjoy the _____ under trees.
9. You may want to _____ a tree.
10. A little tree will grow and become a _____ tree.

Time of Wonder by Robert McCloskey (1958)

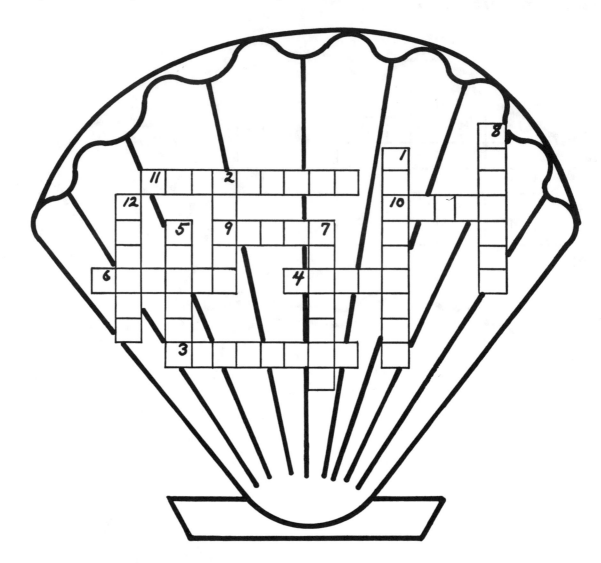

1. The island is located in _____ Bay.
2. On a _____ morning, you feel as though you are standing on the edge of nowhere.
3. The sun shines through and everything _____.
4. During the summer, the bay is spotted with _____.
5. It is fun when _____ come to spend the day.
6. In the evening all is quiet and rather _____.

7. As autumn nears, the days grow _____.
8. Everyone is preparing for some bad _____.
9. The _____ sit solemnly all facing the same direction.
10. The storm lasts most of the _____.
11. The next morning everything looks _____.
12. Summer is over. Time to go home and back to _____.

Name _____   Date _____

Chanticleer and the Fox by Geoffrey Chaucer (1959)   *II–22*
illustrated by Barbara Cooney

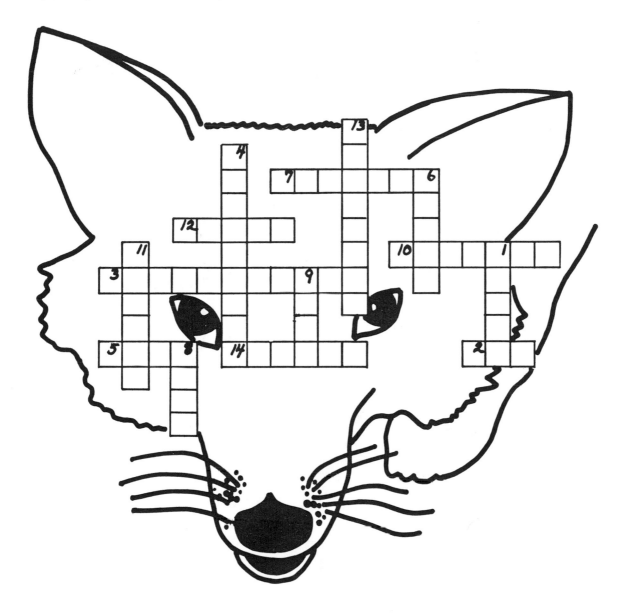

1. The woman was a _____.
2. The woman had _____ daughters.
3. The woman had a rooster named _____.
4. The rooster was considered _____.
5. The rooster had seven _____.
6. The rooster had a very bad _____.
7. The next day a fox _____ into the yard.

8. The fox asked the rooster to _____.
9. When the rooster sang, he closed his
   _____.
10. The fox grabbed the rooster and _____.
11. Everyone _____ the fox.
12. The rooster tricked the fox into opening his
    _____.
13. The rooster told the fox _____ would not
    work again.
14. The rooster learned a valuable _____.

Name _____   Date _____

Nine Days to Christmas by Marie Hall Ets (1960)

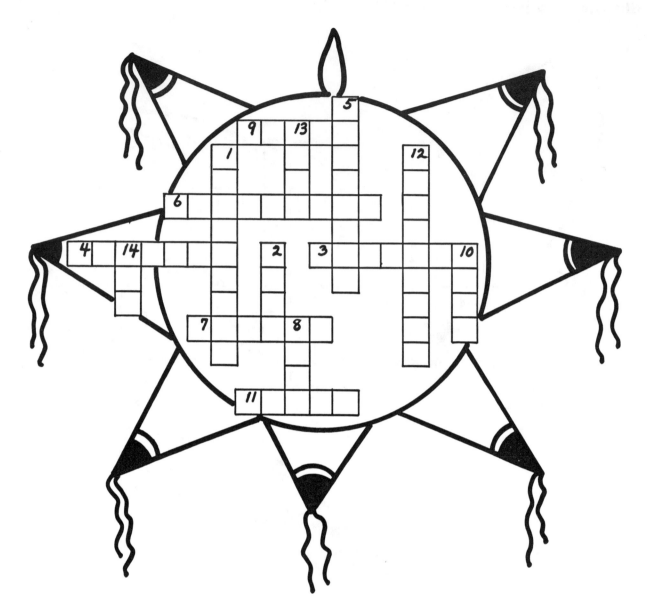

1. The holiday being celebrated is _____.
2. The little girl's name is _____.
3. The special parties before the holiday are called _____.
4. _____ are paper designs with clay pots inside.
5. The little girl's brother's name is _____.
6. Cornflour pancakes are called _____.
7. The little girl's doll's name is _____.

8. The story tells of _____ before the holiday.
9. The servant's name is _____.
10. The design of the little girl's piñata is a _____.
11. Everyone tries to _____ the piñata.
12. A _____ is worn while trying to hit the piñata.
13. The little girl believes her piñata will become a _____ star.
14. The little girl believes she is giving the world a _____.

Name _____   Date _____

Baboushka and the Three Kings by Ruth Robbins (1961)
illustrated by Nicolas Sidjakov

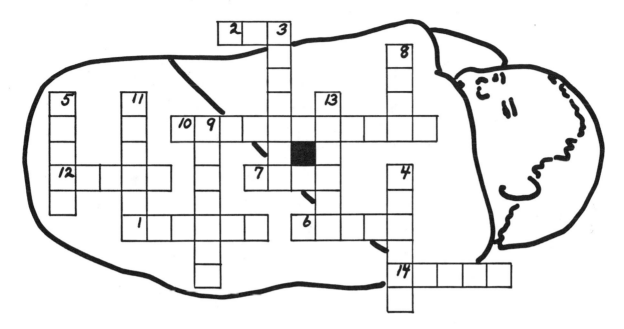

1. The story takes place during the _____.
2. Baboushka was warm and snug in her little _____.
3. She heard a mighty _____ call.
4. Leading a train of travelers was a beautiful _____.
5. Baboushka heard a _____ on her door.
6. Opening the door, she found _____ well-dressed strangers.
7. They told her they were following a bright _____.

8. They were searching for a _____.
9. They _____ Baboushka to go with them.
10. Baboushka declined and the strangers _____ into the storm.
11. Later, Baboushka decided she must _____.
12. She searched, but could not find the _____.
13. Baboushka renews her _____ every year.
14. She never finds the child, but leaves _____ for the children.

Name _____   Date _____

Once a Mouse... by Marcia Brown (1962)

1. A hermit _____ a little mouse caught by a crow.
2. The hermit changes the mouse into different _____.
3. The first change is into a _____.
4. The second change is into a _____.
5. The third change is into a handsome royal _____.
6. The mouse likes this change and becomes very _____.

7. The hermit _____ the beast.
8. The tiger is _____.
9. The tiger plans to _____ the hermit.
10. The hermit reads the tiger's _____.
11. He changes the tiger back into a _____ little mouse.
12. The hermit sits thinking about big and _____.

Name _____   Date _____

The Snowy Day by Ezra Jack Keats (1963)

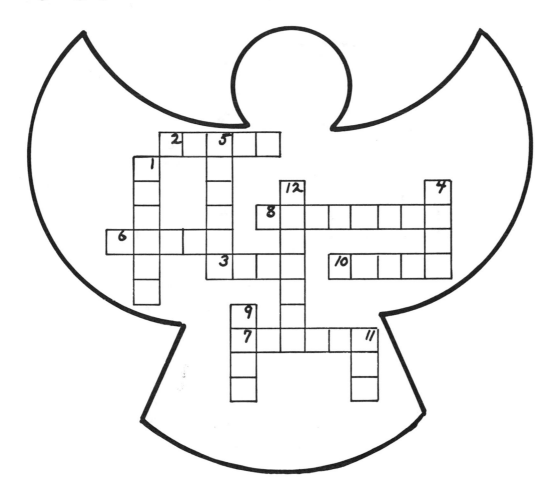

1. The story takes place during the _____.
2. The little boy's name is _____.
3. _____ covered the ground.
4. The little boy went out to _____.
5. First, he made _____ in the snow.
6. He found a _____ and traced it in the snow.

7. Then he made _____ in the snow with his body.
8. He put a _____ in his pocket.
9. He went home and had a warm _____.
10. When he checked his pocket, it was _____.
11. That night, he dreamed the _____ melted the snow.
12. When he woke up, it was _____.

Where the Wild Things Are by Maurice Sendak (1964)

1. One night, Max was wearing his _____.
2. Mother called Max a _____.
3. Max was sent to bed without _____.
4. That night, a _____ grew in Max's room.
5. Max traveled away in a _____.
6. He met some _____ wild things.

7. Max tamed the wild things by _____ at them.
8. The wild things named Max their _____.
9. They had a celebration called a _____.
10. Max was _____. He wanted to go home.
11. The _____ of Max's supper drew him back.
12. Max's supper was waiting. It was still _____.

Name _____   Date _____

May I Bring a Friend? by Beatrice Schenk de Regniers (1965)
illustrated by Beni Montresor

1. The King and Queen invited me to come for tea on _____.
2. I brought my friend, the _____.
3. On Monday, the King and Queen invited me to come and eat _____ for dinner.
4. I brought a hippopotamus, my very _____ friend.
5. The King and Queen invited me for _____ on Tuesday.
6. I brought my friends, the _____.
7. On Wednesday, the King and Queen invited me for _____.
8. I brought my _____, the elephant.
9. The King and Queen invited me for _____ on Thursday.
10. I brought my friends, the _____.
11. I was invited on Friday for _____ Pie Day.
12. I brought my friend, the _____.
13. On Saturday, we all had tea at the _____.

Name _____   Date _____

Always Room for One More by Sorche Nic Leodhas (1966)
illustrated by Nonny Hogrogian

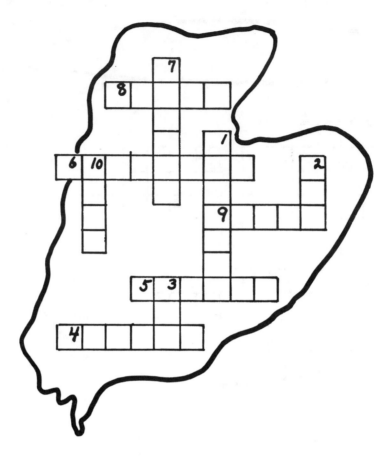

1. The house stood by the _____.
2. It was a _____ little house.
3. _____ children lived in the house.
4. The Scottish word for children is _____.
5. There came a very _____ night.

6. The children's father, Lachie, invited every _____ to come in.
7. The house finally _____ down.
8. Everyone helped Lachie _____ a new house.
9. The new house was _____ as big.
10. Now, there will always be _____ for one more.

Name _____ Date _____

Sam, Bangs and Moonshine by Evaline Ness (1967)

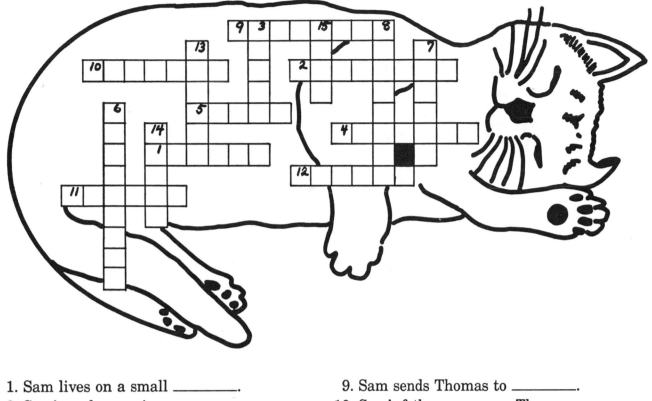

1. Sam lives on a small _____.
2. Sam's real name is _____.
3. Sam has a bad habit of _____.
4. Sam claims her mother is a _____.
5. Sam has a cat named _____.
6. Sam's father calls lying _____.
7. Sam has a friend named _____.
8. He begs to see Sam's baby _____.

9. Sam sends Thomas to _____.
10. Sam's father _____ Thomas.
11. But, Bangs is _____ away.
12. Later, Bangs appears at the _____.
13. Sam's father gives her a _____.
14. Sam _____ the gerbil to Thomas.
15. Now, Sam knows what _____ and moonshine means.

Name _____   Date _____

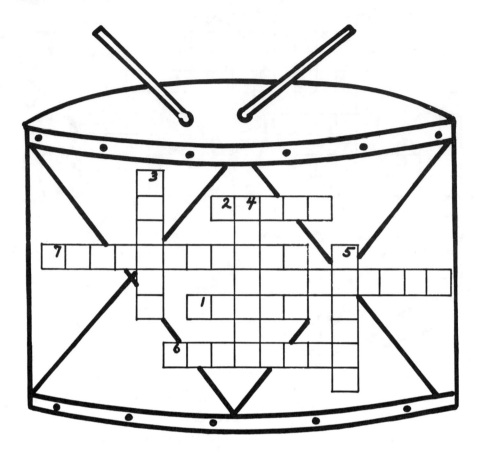

1. The _____ was given by General Border.
2. The shot was brought by Major _____.
3. The _____ was brought by Captain Bammer.
4. The powder was brought by Sergeant _____.

5. The _____ was brought by Corporal Farrell.
6. The carriage was brought by Private _____.
7. But it was fired by _____.
8. Boom went the _____.

Name _____   Date _____

The Fool of the World and the Flying Ship
retold by Arthur Ransome (1969)
illustrated by Uri Shulevitz

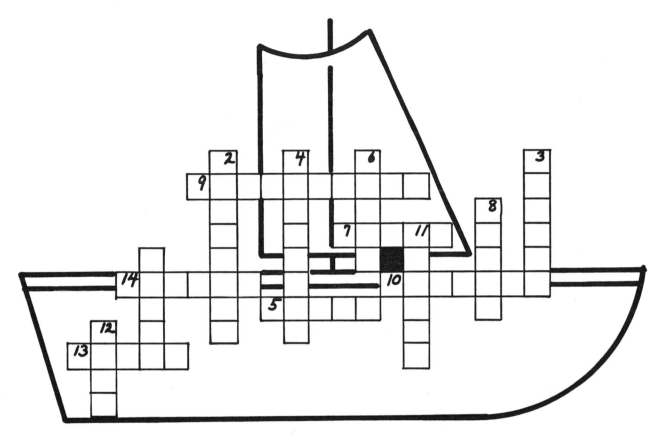

1. A peasant and his wife had _____ sons.
2. The Fool of the World was the _____ son.
3. The czar wanted a _____ ship.
4. In return, he would give his _____ in marriage.
5. The Fool found a ship. He picked up _____ unusual friends and flew to the palace.
6. They weighed anchor in the _____ of the palace.
7. The czar wanted the ship. He tried to _____ the Fool.

8. The czar told the Fool to bring him some _____ water of life.
9. The Fool's unusual _____ helped with three more tasks.
10. The czar agreed that a _____ should take place.
11. Now, everyone thinks the Fool is very _____.
12. Even the czar is _____ of the Fool.
13. And the princess _____ the Fool.
14. All this happened because the Fool _____ his lunch with a very old man.

Name _____   Date _____

Sylvester and the Magic Pebble by William Steig (1970)

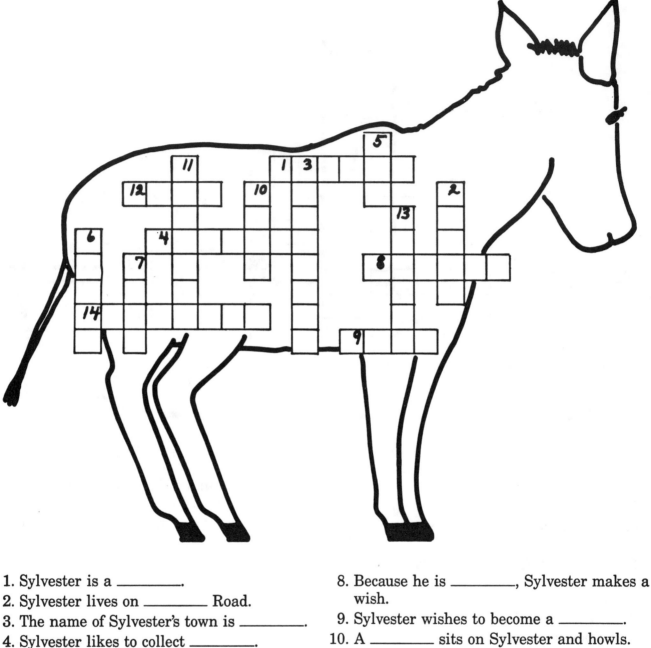

1. Sylvester is a _____.
2. Sylvester lives on _____ Road.
3. The name of Sylvester's town is _____.
4. Sylvester likes to collect _____.
5. He finds a beautiful _____ one.
6. He discovers it is a _____ pebble.
7. On the way home, Sylvester meets a _____.

8. Because he is _____, Sylvester makes a wish.
9. Sylvester wishes to become a _____.
10. A _____ sits on Sylvester and howls.
11. Sylvester's _____ cannot find him anywhere.
12. Sylvester stays under the magic spell for a _____.
13. Finally, Sylvester's parents break the spell when they come to Strawberry Hill for a _____.
14. Sylvester's father puts the pebble in an _____.

Name _____   Date _____

A Story, A Story by Gail E. Haley (1971)   **II—34**

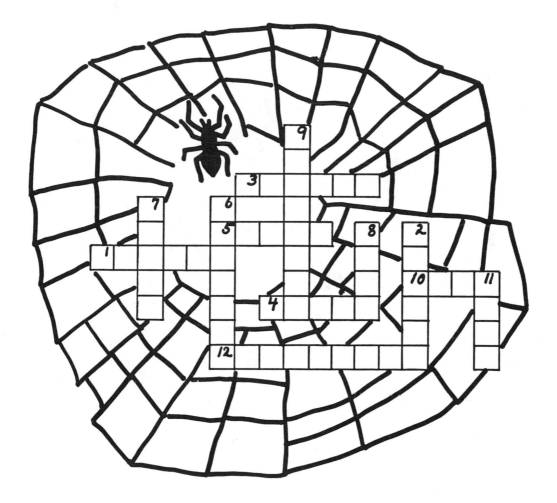

1. Ananse was called a _____ man.
2. Ananse wanted Nyame, the _____'s, stories.
3. Nyame kept the stories in a _____ box.
4. Ananse had to perform _____ tasks.
5. The first task was to capture _____, the leopard.
6. The second task was to capture Mmboro, the _____ that sting like fire.

7. The third task was to capture Mmoatia, the _____.
8. Ananse caught the leopard with the binding _____.
9. Ananse used a _____ to capture the hornets.
10. Ananse used a wooden bowl and _____ to catch the fairy.
11. Ananse _____ a web to the sky to carry the three to Nyame.
12. When Ananse opened the box, the stories _____ to the ends of the world.

Name _____   Date _____

One Fine Day by Nonny Hogrogian (1972)

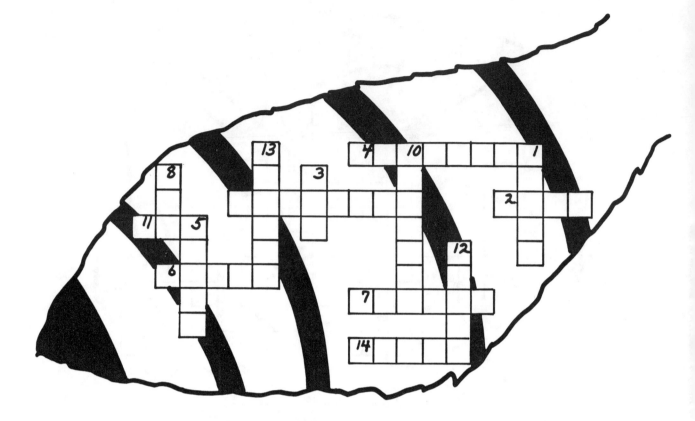

1. A hungry fox _____ the old woman's milk.
2. She was so angry, she cut off his _____.
3. The fox begged her to _____ it back on.
4. She agreed, but only if the fox _____ the milk.
5. The cow wanted _____ in return for some milk.
6. The field wanted _____ in return.
7. The fox tried to get some from the _____.

8. The fox asked a maiden for a _____.
9. She agreed, if he would give her a _____.
10. The fox tried to get one from a _____.
11. But the fox had to get an _____ to pay for it.
12. The hen agreed to exchange one for some _____.
13. The fox was able to get some from a _____.
14. Finally, he brought the milk to the old _____ and she sewed on his tail.

Name _____   Date _____

The Funny Little Woman **by Arlene Mosel (1973)**
illustrated by Blair Lent

1. The setting of the story is old _____.
2. The old woman liked to make _____ dumplings.
3. One day, a dumpling rolled through a _____.
4. The old woman _____ and found an underground road.
5. The road was lined with _____.
6. The old woman called them _____.
7. They warned the old woman of the _____.

8. These bad ones captured the old woman to _____ for them.
9. The old woman stirred the rice with a _____ paddle.
10. The old woman finally escaped by _____.
11. Her captors' plan to catch her failed because she made them _____.
12. The paddle helped the old woman become _____.
13. There are actually two stories in this book, one _____ and one under ground.

Name _____   Date _____

Duffy and the Devil by Harve and Margot Zemach (1974)

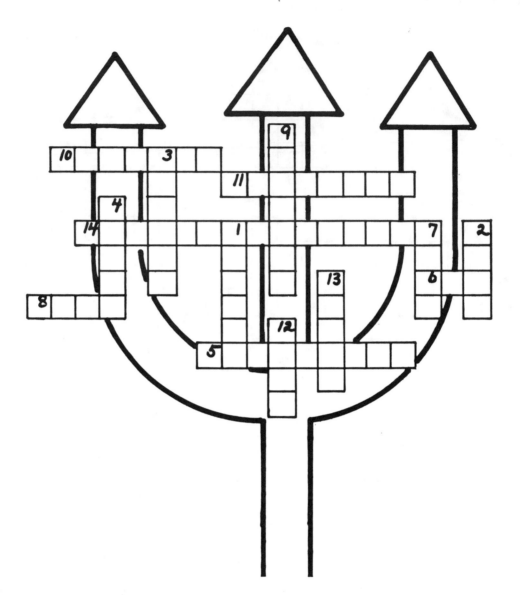

1. This story concerns _____ Lovel of Trove.
2. He had a housekeeper named Old _____.
3. The housekeeper needed a _____.
4. The squire found a girl named _____ to help.
5. The squire thought the girl could spin _____ cloth.
6. The girl could not, and made a bargain with a little _____ to spin the cloth.
7. In return, the girl had to guess his _____.

8. If she could not guess within three years, he would take her _____.
9. The squire _____ the girl.
10. The squire came upon some _____ in a cavern.
11. He told the girl of a funny little man named _____.
12. When the girl called the man's name, the squire's clothes turned to _____.
13. The little man was really the _____.
14. This story is similar to the story titled _____.

Name _____   Date _____

Arrow to the Sun by Gerald McDermott (1975)

1. This story is a _____ Indian folktale.
2. The Lord of the Sun sent the _____ to earth and the boy was born.
3. The boy was teased for he had no _____.
4. The boy left home. He met _____.
5. Later, he met _____.
6. The boy became an _____.
7. He traveled to the _____.

8. He passed through the kiva of _____.
9. And then the kiva of _____.
10. And then the kiva of _____.
11. And finally, the kiva of _____.
12. The boy was filled with _____.
13. The boy returned to _____.
14. He joined in the _____ of life.

Name _____   Date _____

Why Mosquitoes Buzz in People's Ears by Verna Aardema (1976)
illustrated by Leo and Diane Dillon

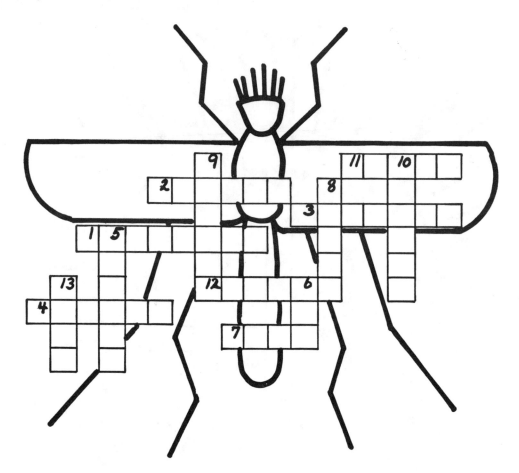

1. The _____ started it all.
2. The _____ stuck two sticks in his ears.
3. That scared the python who hid in _____ hole.
4. Rabbit's running caused crow to _____ the alarm.
5. The excited monkey broke a branch which fell and killed one of the _____.
6. Mother Owl was so unhappy, she would not wake the _____.
7. King _____ called all the animals together.

8. Each animal said it was not his _____.
9. Then they called, "_____ the mosquito."
10. To this day, the mosquito has a _____ conscience.
11. The mosquito keeps asking, "Is everyone still _____ at me?"
12. The mosquito gets an _____ answer.
13. The answer is _____.

Name _____   Date _____

Ashanti to Zulu by Margaret Musgrove (1977)   **II—40**
illustrated by Leo and Diane Dillon

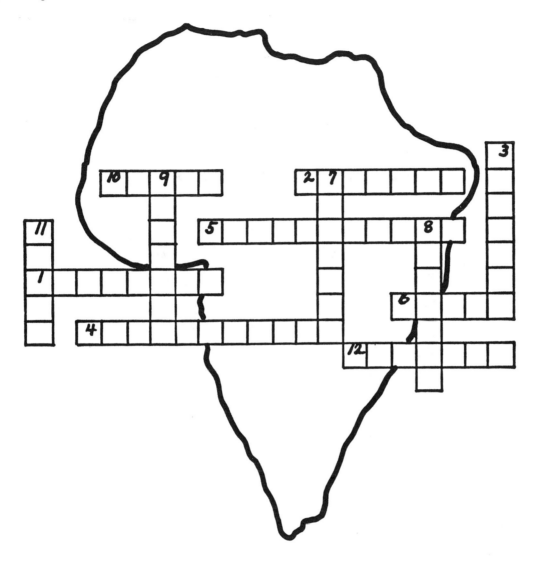

1. Ashanti to Zulu is an _____ book.
2. Ashanti to Zulu is all about _____ tribes.
3. The book tells of the _____ of the tribes.
4. Many of the ways of the tribes are very _____.
5. The Ewe people talk with _____.

6. The Jie men roam with the cattle and the women do the _____.
7. The Kung people store water in _____ eggshells.
8. The Rendille people live in _____ houses.
9. In the Tuareg tribe, the _____ are the storytellers.
10. The Vai people carry everything on their _____.
11. The Zulus are great _____.

Name _____   Date _____

Noah's Ark by Peter Spier (1978)

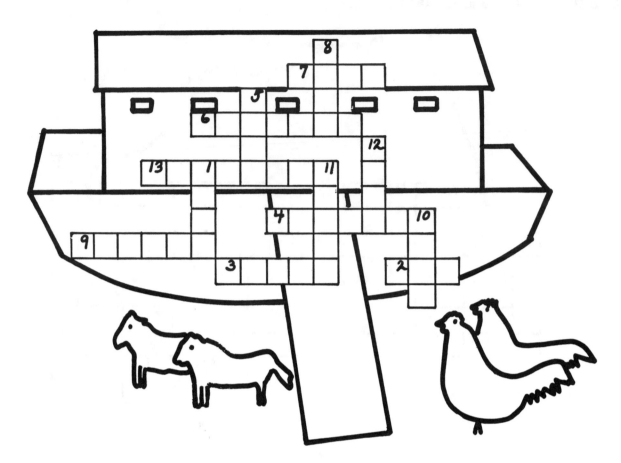

1. The ark was built by _____ and his family.
2. The animals came in two by _____.
3. The _____ came.
4. The land was _____.
5. Life was _____ inside the ark.
6. _____ and lightning stormed the ark.
7. The ark became stranded on a _____.

8. Noah released a white _____.
9. The bird brought back a small _____.
10. Noah knew the flood waters were going _____.
11. Noah opened the side _____ of the ark.
12. All were happy to be on _____ again.
13. Noah planted a _____.

The Girl Who Loved Wild Horses by Paul Goble (1979)   *II—42*

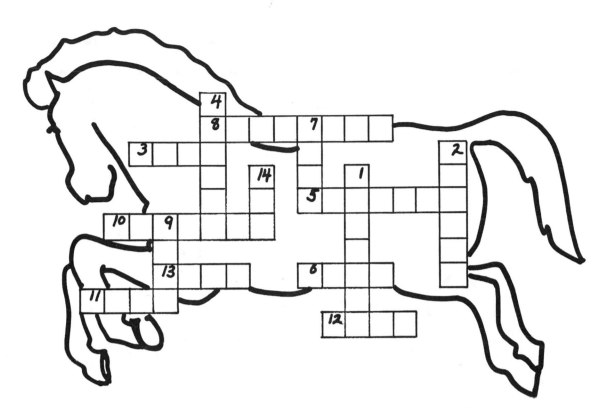

1. The people followed the _____.
2. The people used _____ to carry their belongings.
3. There was a _____ in the village who understood horses.
4. The girl fell _____ one day.
5. A terrible _____ storm shook the valley.
6. The girl and the horses ran _____.
7. They became _____.

8. The _____ welcomed them.
9. Finally, hunters found the girl and brought her _____.
10. The girl became very _____.
11. She returned to _____ with the horses.
12. Every year, she brought her parents a _____.
13. One year she did not come. The people believed she had become a _____.
14. The people felt great _____.

Ox-Cart Man by Donald Hall (1980)
illustrated by Barbara Cooney

1. In the month of _____ he backed his ox into his cart.
2. His _____ packed the cart with homemade and home-grown items.
3. He walked for _____ days through the countryside.
4. He finally arrived at Portsmouth _____.
5. He sold _____.
6. He even sold the ox and _____ him goodbye on the nose.
7. His pockets were full of _____.

8. He bought an iron _____ to hang over the fireplace.
9. He bought his daughter an embroidery _____.
10. He bought his son a Barlow _____.
11. He bought wintergreen peppermint _____ for everyone.
12. He walked _____ with his purchases.
13. That night, he began stitching a new _____ for the young ox in the barn.

Name _____   Date _____

Fables by Arnold Lobel (1981)

1. The fables in this book are all about
   _____.
2. A fable has a _____ at the end of the
   story.
3. The cover shows the illustration from The
   _____ and the Crow.
4. In fables, one character often _____ the
   other.
5. Fables often point out that people are
   _____.
6. One fable tells us that children often
   reflect their _____.

7. Another fable tells us that a change of
   _____ can be healthful.
8. The story of The Hen and the _____ Tree
   is funny.
9. Three frogs went searching for the end of
   the _____ but found a snake instead.
10. The camel who wished to be a _____
    dancer pleased only herself.
11. The pelican had no friends because of his
    bad _____.
12. The hippopotamus was stuck at the table
    because he was _____.

Jumanji **by Chris Van Allsburg (1982)**

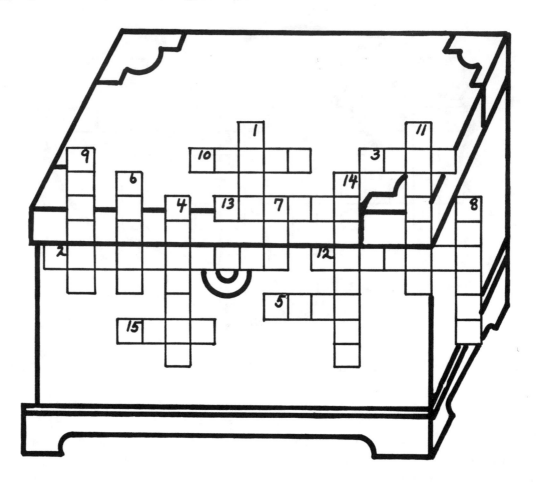

1. Judy and Peter found a _____ in the park.
2. Once started, the players cannot stop until one player reaches the _____.
3. Peter's first turn produced a _____.
4. Judy's first turn produced a dozen _____.
5. Peter's next turn produced _____.
6. On Judy's next turn, a lost _____ appeared.
7. Peter was bitten by a tsetse _____ and fell asleep.
8. Judy landed on a space that produced a herd of _____.

9. Peter's space read, "A _____ sneaks into camp."
10. Judy was safe for a bit when she landed on a _____ space.
11. Peter's next space read, "_____ erupts."
12. Judy frantically made it to the city and yelled "_____."
13. Everything became as it was _____.
14. The children quickly _____ the game to the park.
15. Later, they saw two _____ running through the park carrying a box.

Name _____ Date _____

adapted and illustrated by Marcia Brown

1. Shadow itself has no _____.
2. Shadow is mute. Shadow has no _____.
3. Shadow does not sleep. Shadow is always
   _____.
4. In the light, Shadow is _____.
5. In the dark, Shadow is _____.
6. Shadow asks for nothing. Shadow knows no
   _____.

7. Be careful. Shadow can cast a _____ over
   you.
8. The zebra's shadow has no _____.
9. Shadow is quiet when _____ falls.
10. No one can _____ Shadow.
11. In the daytime, Shadow is full of _____.
12. Shadow is _____.

The Glorious Flight by Alice and Martin Provensen (1984)

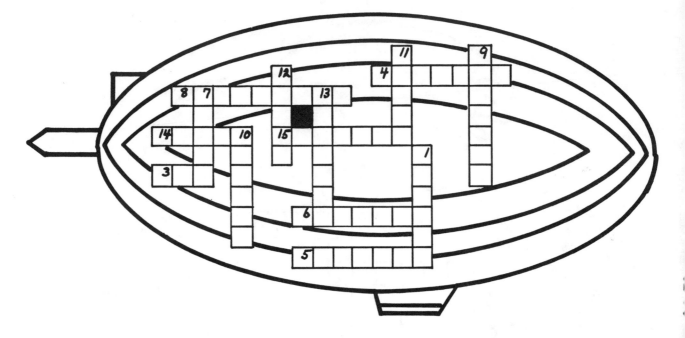

1. **(down) The story begins in the city of Cambrai in _____.**

1. **(across) Mr. Louis Blériot has a wife and _____ children.**

3. The family goes for a ride in their shiny new _____.

4. A great white _____ is spotted overhead.

5. Mr. Blériot decides to build a flying _____.

6. The Blériot I flaps like a _____.

7. The Blériot II crashes into the _____.

8. The Blériot III has a motor and a

_____.

9. The Blériot IV flies around in _____.

10. The Blériot V hops about like a _____.

11. The Blériot VI flies across a _____.

12. The Blériot VII really _____.

13. Mr. Blériot enters a contest to fly across the _____ Channel.

14. Mr. Blériot finally sees the white cliffs of

_____.

15. Mr. Blériot successfully lands in _____.

Saint George and the Dragon by Margaret Hodges (1985)
illustrated by Trina Schart Hyman

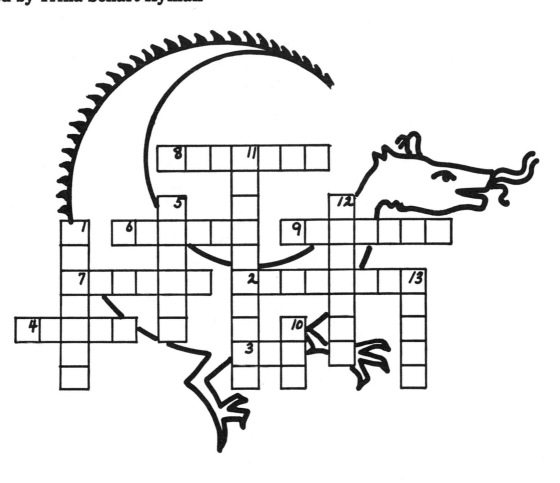

1. The setting of the story is ancient _____.
2. The _____ Knight was riding into his first battle.
3. Princess _____ rode beside him on a little white donkey.
4. Behind her, a _____ followed, carrying food.
5. They were returning to the princess's land to fight a _____.
6. During the long ride, they stopped and rested at the home of a _____.
7. Here, the knight learned that his name was _____.

8. After the first battle with the dragon, the knight was revived with water from a _____ spring.
9. After the second battle, the knight's wounds were eased by a _____ dew from an apple tree.
10. The knight finally killed the dragon by running his sword through the dragon's open _____.
11. The people came to praise the _____ knight.
12. The knight and the princess were _____.
13. The knight finally earned the title, _____ George of Merry England.

The Polar Express by Chris Van Allsburg (1986)

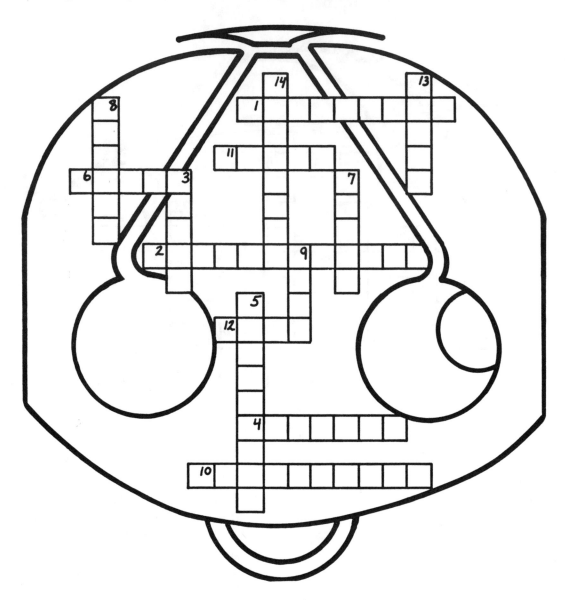

1. The story takes place on _____ Eve.
2. I was listening for the sound of _____.
3. I saw a _____ stopped in front of my house.
4. The train was filled with children wearing _____ and nightgowns.
5. We traveled to the _____.
6. One of us would be chosen to receive the _____ gift of Christmas.
7. The streets of the center of the North Pole were filled with _____.

8. In the middle of a large circle stood Santa's _____.
9. Santa chose me to receive the first _____ of Christmas.
10. All I wanted was one _____.
11. After Santa left, we trooped back into the _____ Express.
12. I discovered I had _____ the silver bell.
13. But, _____ found the silver bell and left it behind the tree.
14. Only _____ can hear the ringing of the silver bell.

Name _____   Date _____

Hey, Al by Arthur Yorinks (1987)
illustrated by Richard Egielski   *II—50*

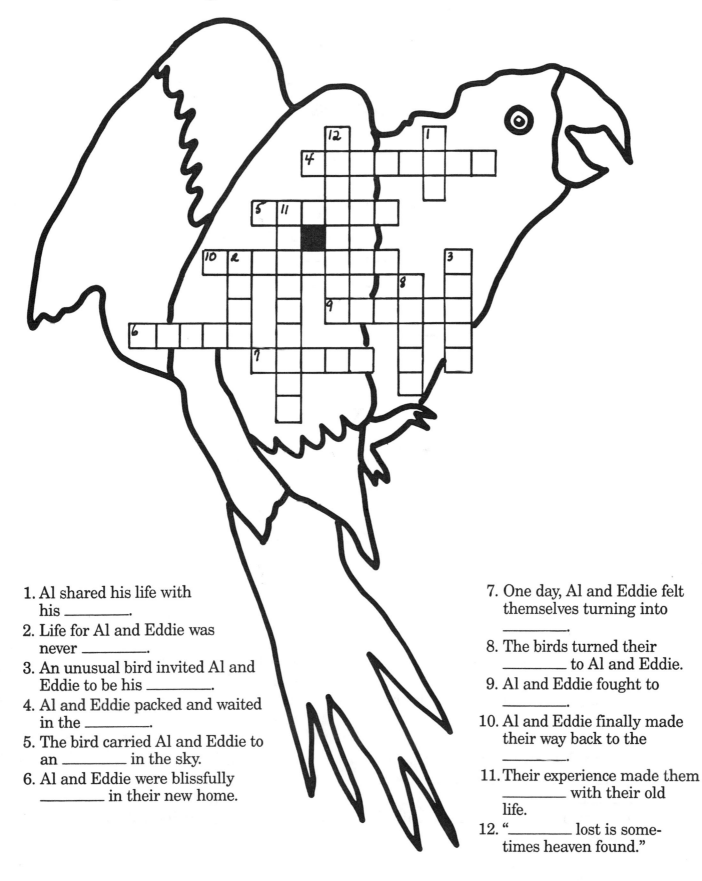

1. Al shared his life with his _____.
2. Life for Al and Eddie was never _____.
3. An unusual bird invited Al and Eddie to be his _____.
4. Al and Eddie packed and waited in the _____.
5. The bird carried Al and Eddie to an _____ in the sky.
6. Al and Eddie were blissfully _____ in their new home.

7. One day, Al and Eddie felt themselves turning into _____.
8. The birds turned their _____ to Al and Eddie.
9. Al and Eddie fought to _____.
10. Al and Eddie finally made their way back to the _____.
11. Their experience made them _____ with their old life.
12. "_____ lost is sometimes heaven found."

Name _____   Date _____

Owl Moon by Jane Yolan (1988)   *II-51*
illustrated by John Schoenherr

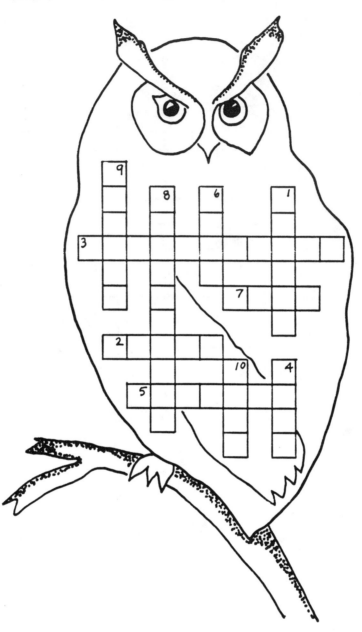

1. Pa and I went owling late one _____ night.
2. When you go owling, you must be _____.
3. Pa made the sound of a _____ owl.
4. My brothers had said, sometimes there's an owl and sometimes there _____.
5. In the woods, the _____ stained the white snow.
6. Pa called again and an _____ came back.
7. The owl _____ right over our heads.
8. Pa caught the owl in the beam of his _____.
9. The owl, Pa and I _____ at one another.
10. When you go owling, all you need is _____.

Name _____   Date _____

Song and Dance Man by Karen Ackerman (1989)   **II-52**
illustrated by Stephen Gammell

1. Grandpa used to sing and dance on the _____ stage.
2. One day, he takes us to the _____.
3. Grandpa opens a brown, leather trimmed _____.
4. Grandpa takes out his tap shoes and wipes them with a _____.
5. Grandpa puts on a _____ for us.
6. Grandpa sings and dances and performs _____ tricks.
7. We laugh so hard that we get the _____.
8. Grandpa turns the lights down low for the _____.
9. It is a wonderful act of _____, spinning, and jumping.
10. We clap and shout for _____, but Grandpa has finished.
11. Grandpa puts everything _____ away in the trunk.
12. Grandpa loves being with us, but we know he _____ being on the stage.

Name _____   Date _____

Lon Po Po by Ed Young (1990)

1. Three _____ girls lived in the country with their mother.
2. Their names were _____, Tao, and Paotze.
3. Mother went away to visit the girls' grandmother, _____.
4. Mother warned the girls to close and the latch the door at _____.
5. A _____ tricked the girls into opening the door.
6. The girls offered to pick the animal some magic _____ nuts.
7. Once safe in the tree, they offered to pull the animal up in a _____.
8. _____ times, they pulled the rope part way up and let it drop.
9. The last fall broke the animal's _____.
10. The girls locked the door and fell peacefully _____.

Name _____   Date _____

Black and White by David Macauley (1991)

1. This book can be one story or _____ stories.
2. This book has sub-titles. The first is _____ Things.
3. The second is Problem _____.
4. The third is A _____ Game.
5. The last is _____ Chaos.
6. Two main things appear through this book. One is _____.

7. The other is _____.
8. Two main colors appear through this book. One is _____.
9. The other is _____.
10. The story is seen through the eyes and mind of a young _____.
11. This book depends upon the _____ understanding.
12. To appreciate this book, one must read it _____ times.

Name _____ Date _____

Tuesday by David Wiesner (1992)

1. The story begins Tuesday evening
   around _____ o'clock.
2. The frogs take off on _____.
3. At 11:21 PM, they startle a man
   eating a _____.
4. The frogs tangle with _____
   on the clothesline.
5. They fly into a _____.

6. The frogs watch _____ for
   a while.
7. At 4:38 AM, a _____ turns tail
   and flees.
8. At dawn, the frogs return to the
   _____.
9. They leave behind a _____.
10. Next Tuesday at 7:58 PM, will
    _____ fly?

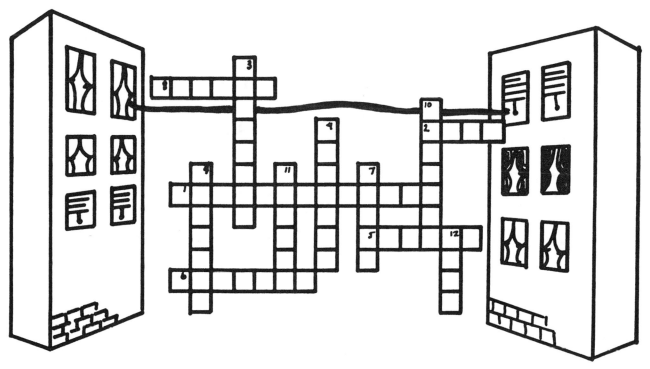

1. Mirette and her mother ran a _____ on English Street.
2. A stranger named Bellini came for a _____.
3. Mirette discovered he is a _____ walker.
4. Mirette's feet _____ to join Bellini on the high wire.
5. She taught herself to walk the _____ of the wire.
6. Bellini agreed to become her _____.

7. Mirette discovered Bellini is _____ famous.
8. He has retired because he has become _____.
9. Bellini knew he must _____ his fear.
10. He stepped out onto the wire and _____.
11. Mirette joined him on the wire. They met in the _____.
12. Mirette and Bellini become a famous _____.

Answer Keys

The following pages provide complete answer keys for the Newbery and Caldecott puzzles in Sections I and II.

SECTION I

Do You Know the Newbery Award Titles?

1. *Smoky the Cowhorse*   *It's Like This, Cat*
   The Cat Who Went to Heaven   *Shadow of a Bull*
   The White Stag   *Mrs. Frisby and the Rats of NIMH*
   Rabbit Hill   *Julie of the Wolves*

2. *Summer of the Swans*
   The Witch of Blackbird Pond

3. *Summer of the Swans*
   Thimble Summer

4. *The Matchlock Gun*   *Rifles for Watie*
   The Bronze Bow

5. *Onion John*

6. *Strawberry Girl*

7. *Ginger Pye*

8. *Hitty, Her First Hundred Years* *Caddie Woodlawn*
   Invincible Louisa   *Julie of the Wolves*
   Dicey's Song   *Sarah, Plain and Tall*

9. *Daniel Boone*   *And Now Miguel*
   Adam of the Road   *Rifles for Watie*
   Johnny Tremain   *Onion John*
   Amos Fortune, Free Man   *I, Juan de Pareja*
   Jacob Have I Loved

10. *Voyages of Doctor Dolittle*   *Young Fu of the Upper Yangtze*
    Tales from Silver Lands   *Secret of the Andes*
    The Trumpeter of Krakow   *I, Juan de Pareja*

11. *Tales from Silver Lands*   *Island of the Blue Dolphins*
    The Bronze Bow   *The Witch of Blackbird Pond*

12. *King of the Wind*   *The High King*
    The Grey King

13. *Hitty, Her First Hundred Years*
    The Twenty-One Balloons

14. *A Gathering of Days*

15. *Miss Hickory*   *Mrs. Frisby and the Rats of NIMH*
    From the Mixed-Up Files of Mrs.
       Basil E. Frankweiler

16. *The Story of Mankind*

17. *Dear Mr. Henshaw*
    Carry On, Mr. Bowditch

18. *Dobry*
19. *From the Mixed-Up Files of Mrs. Basil E. Frankweiler*
20. *King of the Wind*
    Roll of Thunder, Hear My Cry
21. *A Wrinkle in Time*
22. *Shen of the Sea*   *Miracles on Maple Hill*
    Waterless Mountain   *The Witch of Blackbird Pond*
    Rabbit Hill   *Island of the Blue Dolphin*
23. *The Wheel on the School*
    Roller Skates
24. *Thimble Summer*
25. *The Hero and the Crown*
26. *Dicey's Song*
    The Trumpeter of Krakow
27. *A Visit to William Blake's Inn*
    Tales from Silver Lands
28. *Jacob Have I loved*
    Dear Mr. Henshaw
29. *The Westing Game*
30. *M. C. Higgins the Great*
    From the Mixed-Up Files of Mrs. Basil E. Frankweiler

SECTION I: NEWBERY AWARD ANSWER KEY

I–1 *The Story of Mankind*

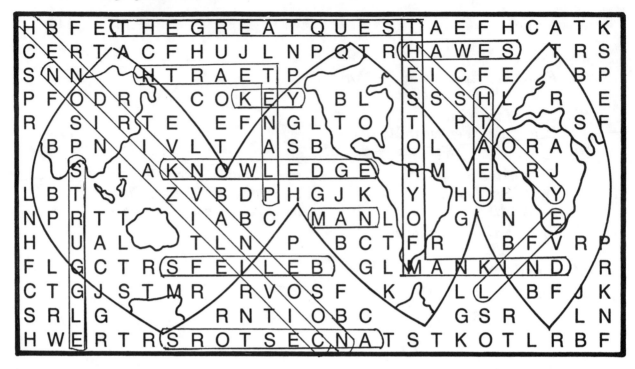

I–2 *The Voyages of Doctor Dolittle*

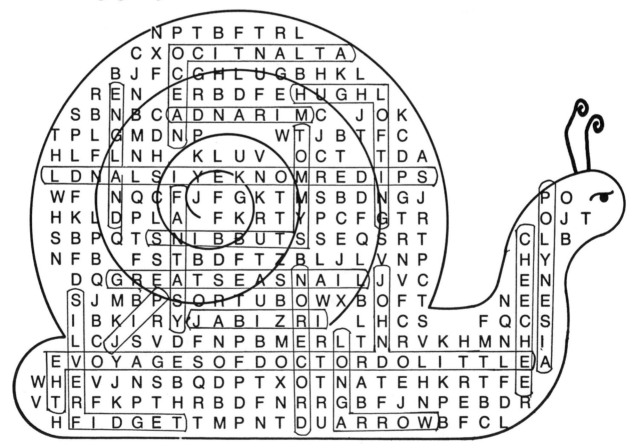

I–3 The Dark Frigate

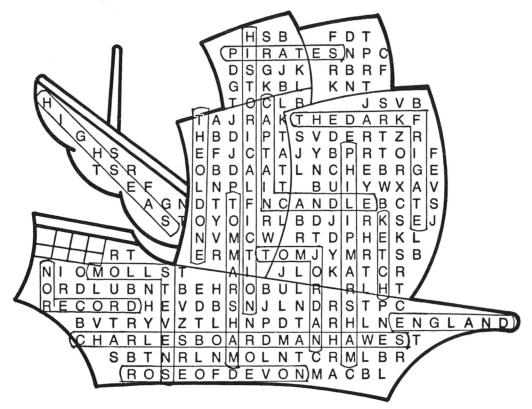

I–4 Tales from Silver Lands

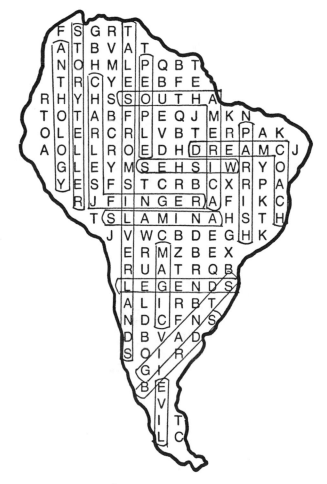

I–5 Shen of the Sea

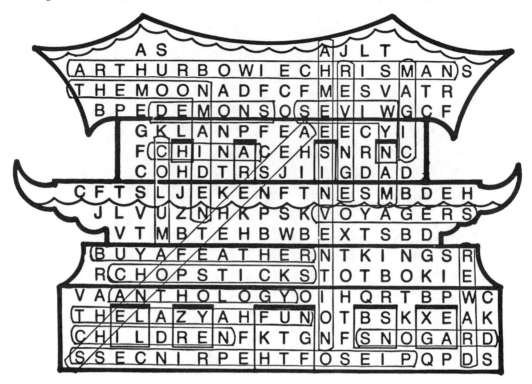

I–6 Smoky the Cowhorse

I–7 Gay-Neck, the Story of a Pigeon

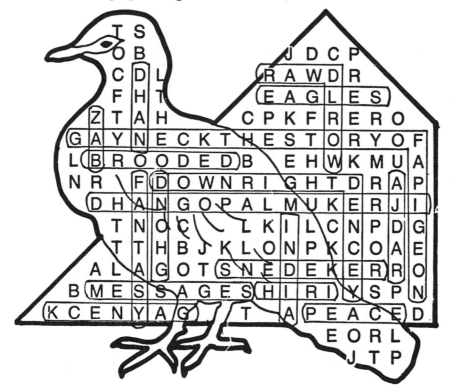

I–8 The Trumpeter of Krakow

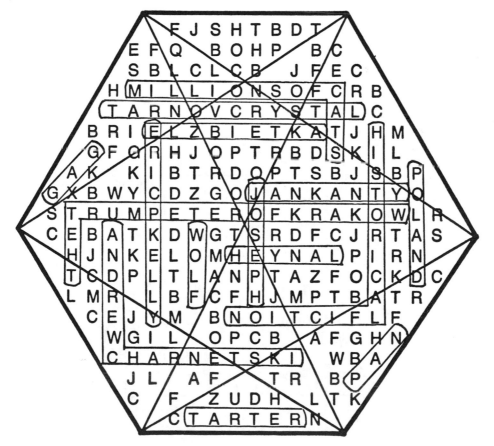

I—9 *Hitty, Her First Hundred Years*

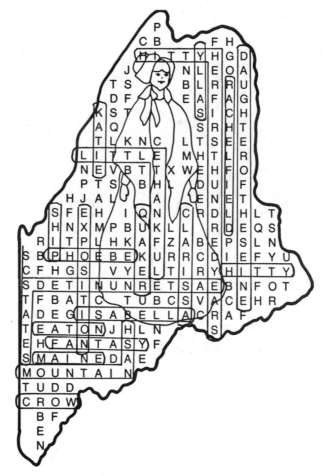

I—10 *The Cat Who Went to Heaven*

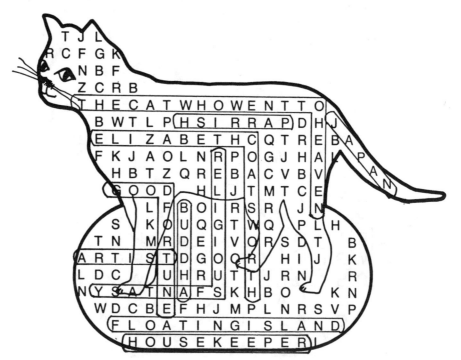

I–11 Waterless Mountain

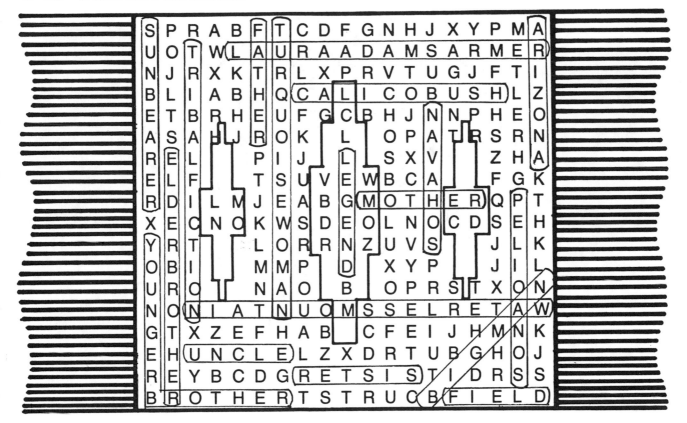

I–12 Young Fu of the Upper Yangtze

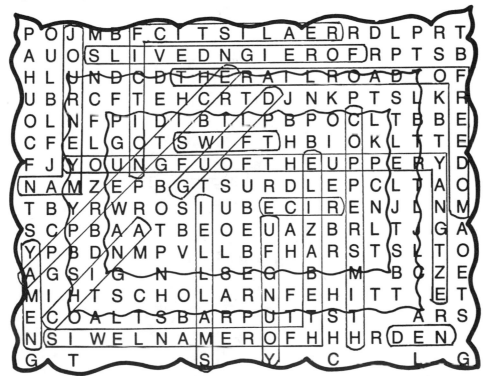

I—13 Invincible Louisa

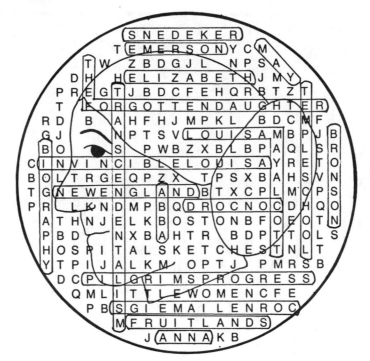

I—14 Dobry

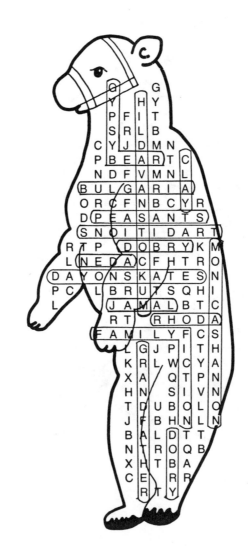

I–15 *Caddie Woodlawn*

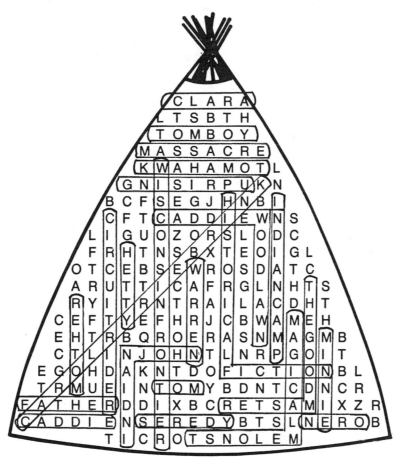

I–16 *Roller Skates*

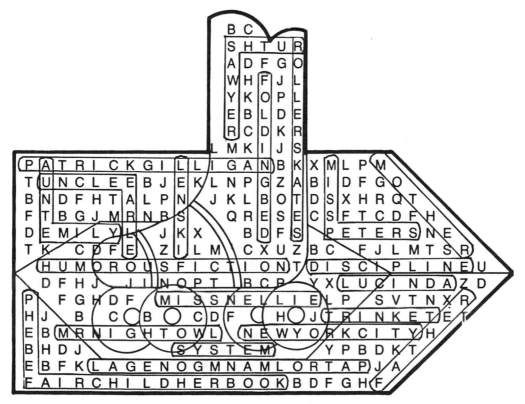

I-17 The White Stag

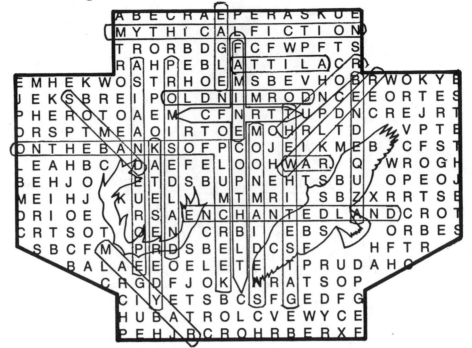

I-18 Thimble Summer

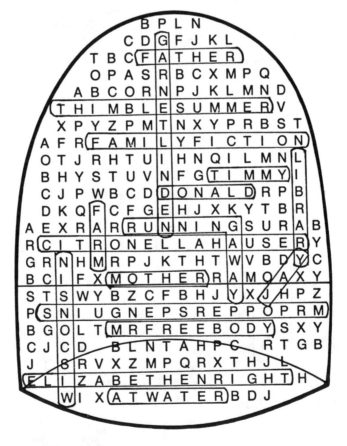

I-19 Daniel Boone

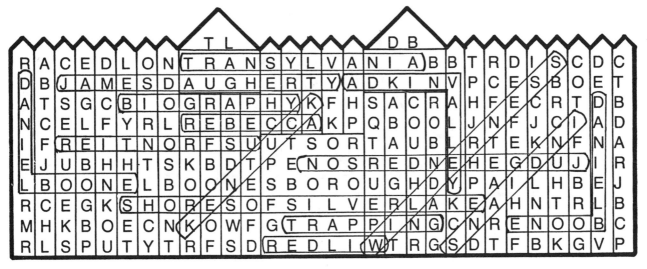

I-20 Call It Courage

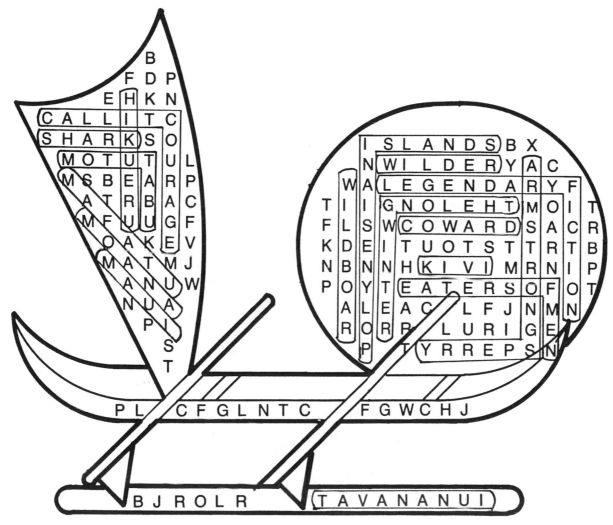

I–21 *The Matchlock Gun*

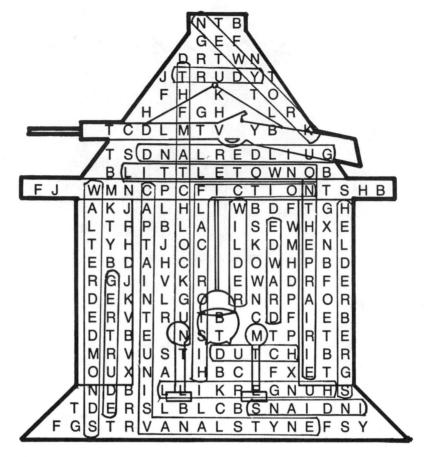

I–22 *Adam of the Road*

I—23 Johnny Tremain

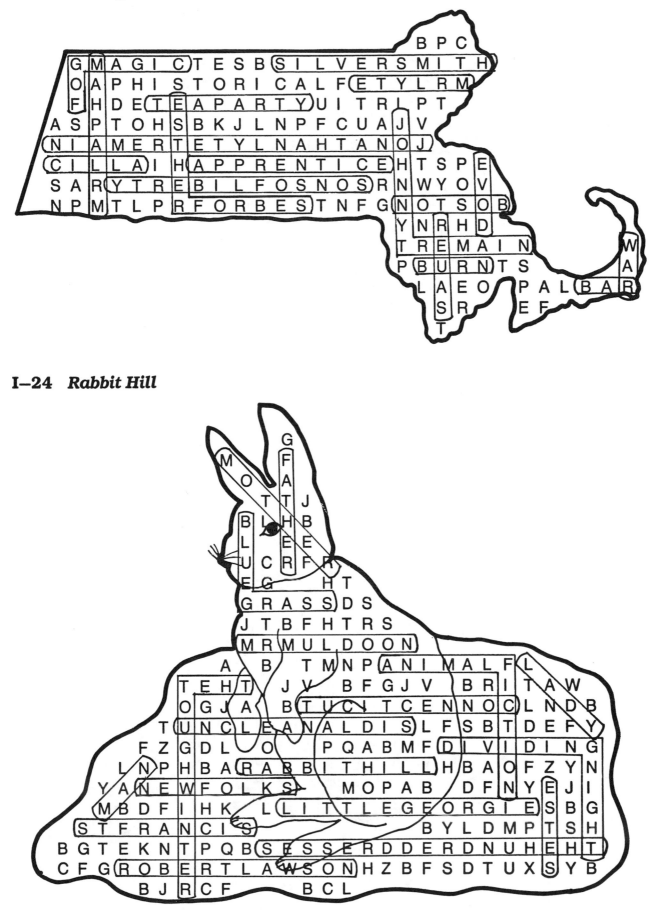

I—24 Rabbit Hill

I–25 Strawberry Girl

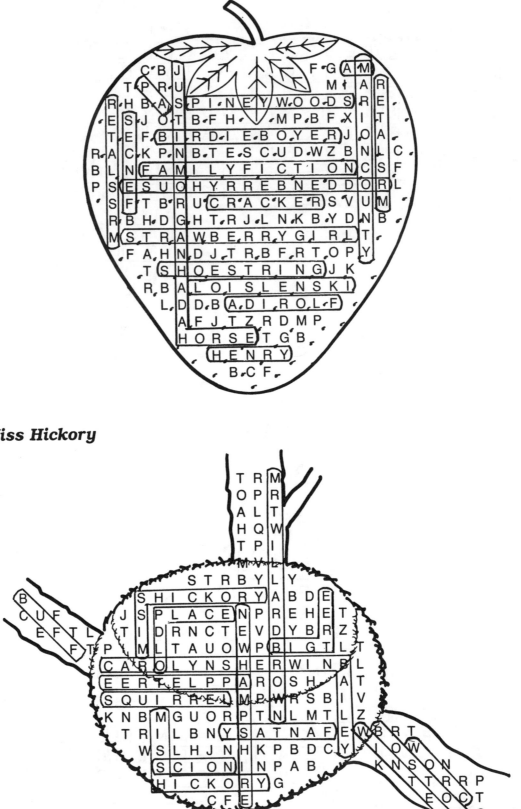

I–26 Miss Hickory

I-27 The Twenty-One Balloons

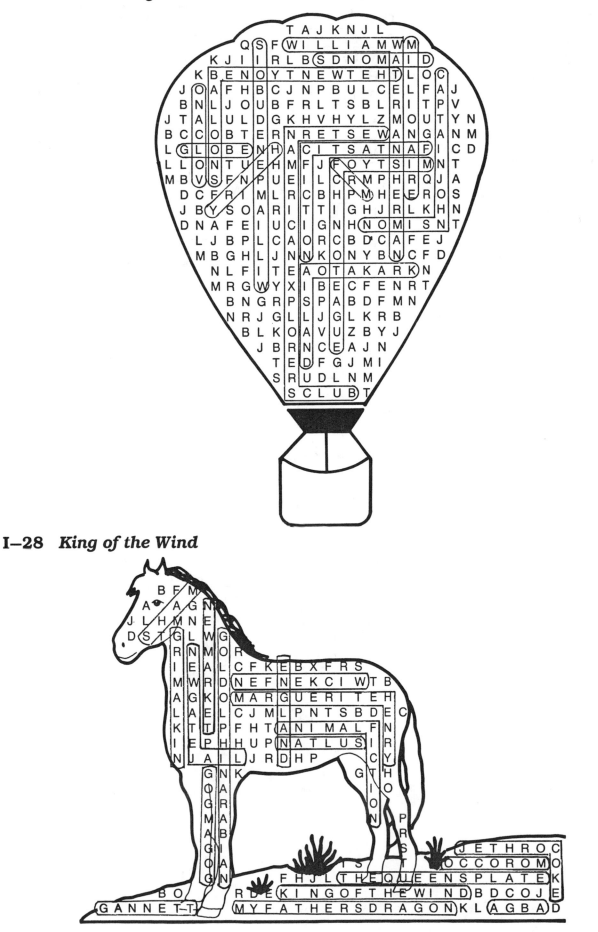

I-28 King of the Wind

I—29 *The Door in the Wall*

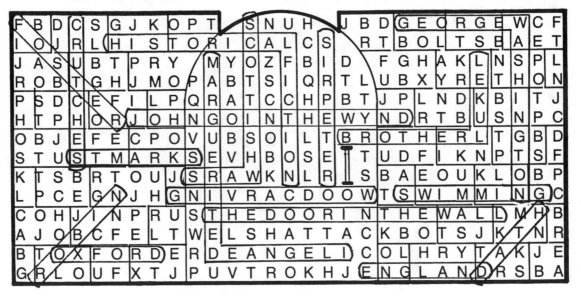

I—30 *Amos Fortune, Free Man*

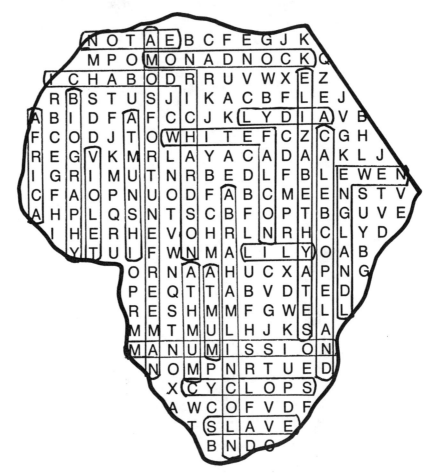

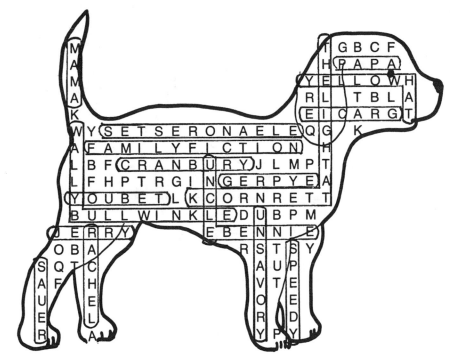

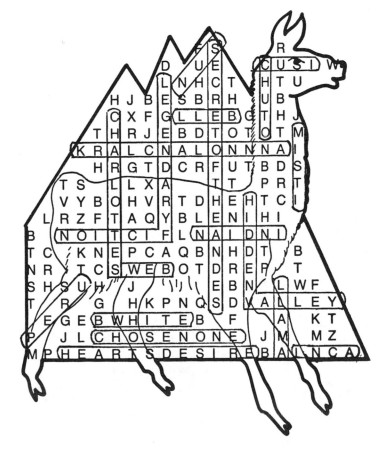

I-33 And Now Miguel

I-34 The Wheel on the School

I–35 *Carry On, Mr. Bowditch*

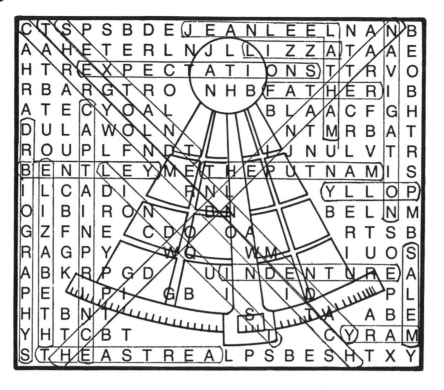

I–36 *Miracles on Maple Hill*

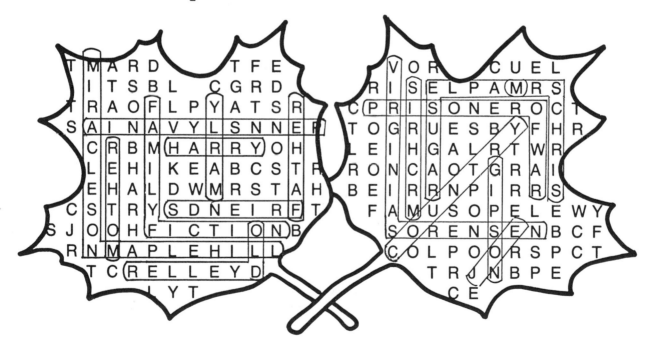

I—37 Rifles for Watie

```
A T S B R K J E F F E R S O N D
H P B M N L T Q B A D T I J R A
A V T R S B D H K N P R L T O V
R E P E A T I N G R I F L E S I
O W Y T S A F E J M D T B C J S
L R L W N P M S R I F L E S F B
D A Q R B F N N S V A L R F O U
K A N S A S V O L U N T E E R S
E E O N T R L A V X Z B Y A W S
I L R J L K B H K D M N B F A E
T R J K U O L B A B B I T T T Y
H D F E C K V D C E T F L M I T
Q A R Z Y W A S H B O U R N E B
```

```
G O N E A W A Y L A K E Y
A L A C I R O T S I H D B
F U R T G E N E R A L A
M I X N D T B A D W
I C T O T I B R L T A T
D I O S B R O T C X Y B T E
D L B O Z N P L M N I R
L E N H A K M R T B T
W E S T F B F E E R
B P D X Y D R B Z
Q A L N T H G I R N E T
C R B T H K B R L Z L
```

I—38 The Witch of Blackbird Pond

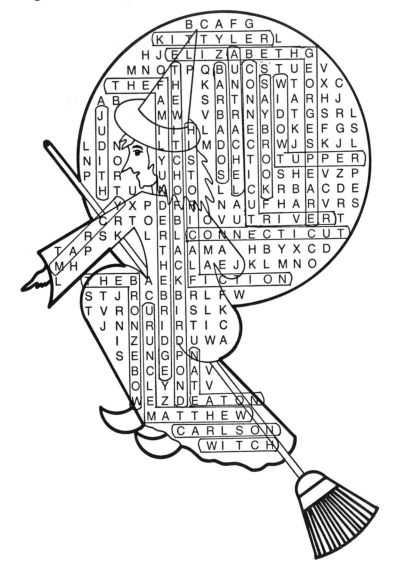

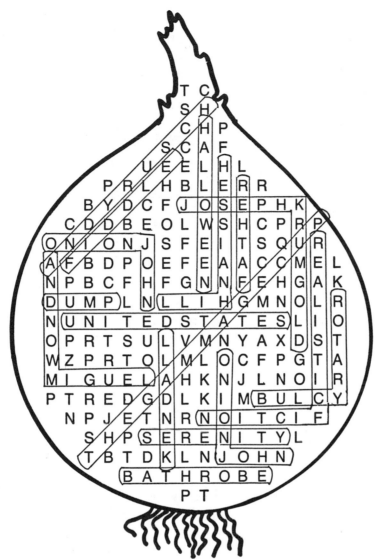

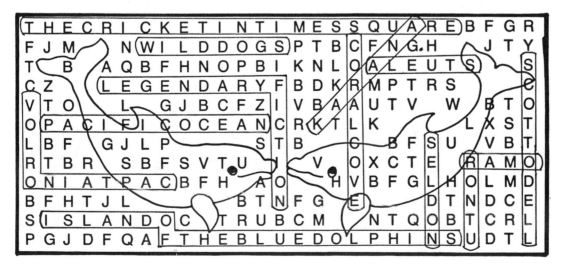

I—41 *The Bronze Bow*

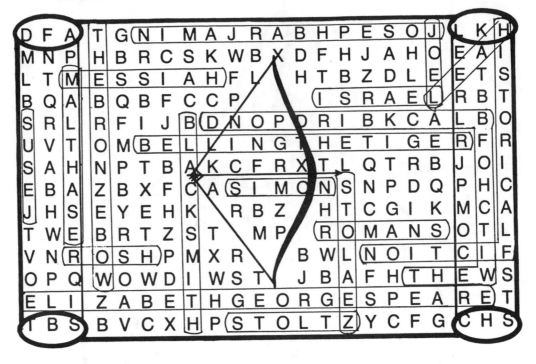

I—42 *A Wrinkle in Time*

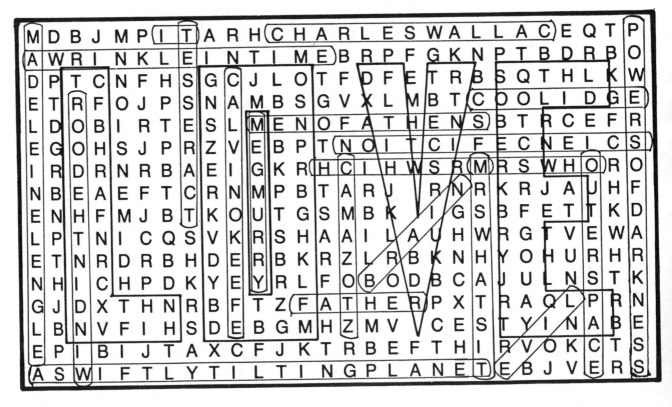

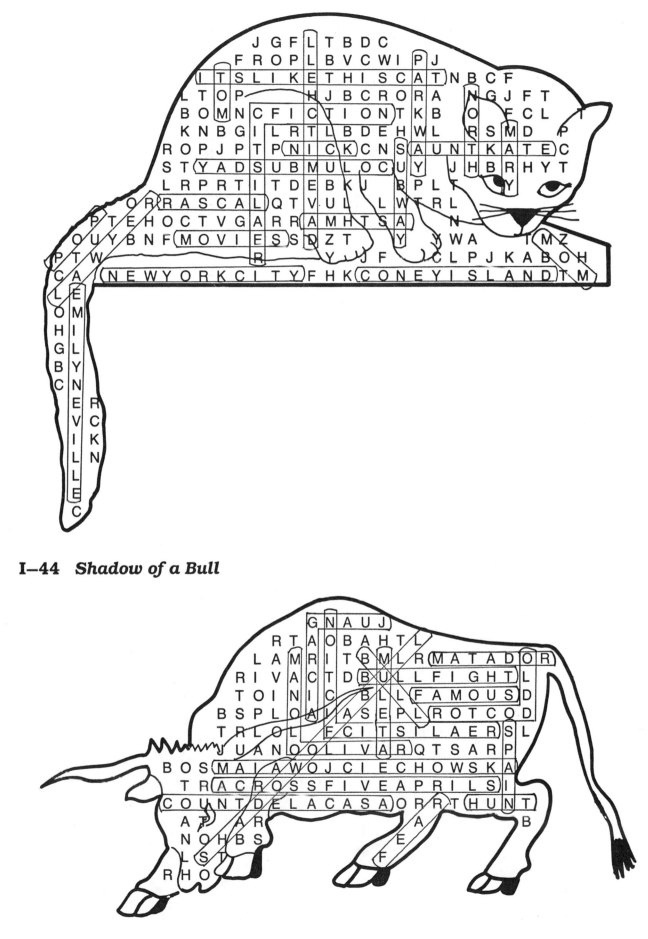

I–45 I, Juan de Pareja

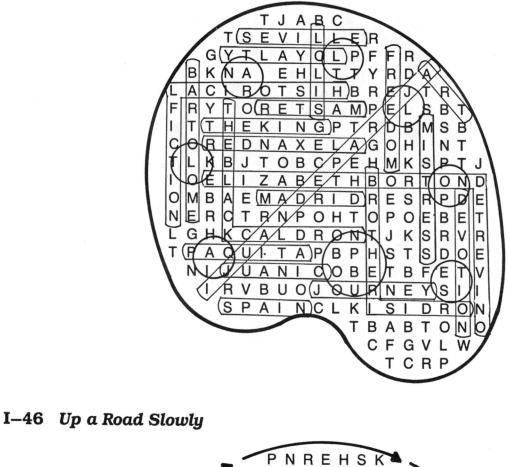

I–46 Up a Road Slowly

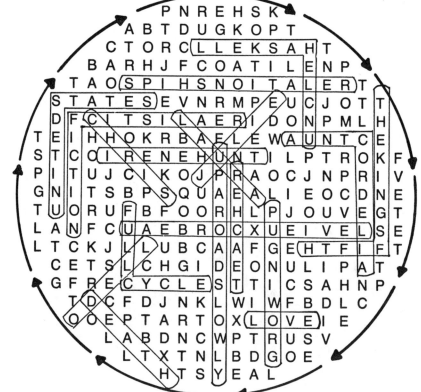

I—47 *From the Mixed-up Files of Mrs. Basil E. Frankweiler*

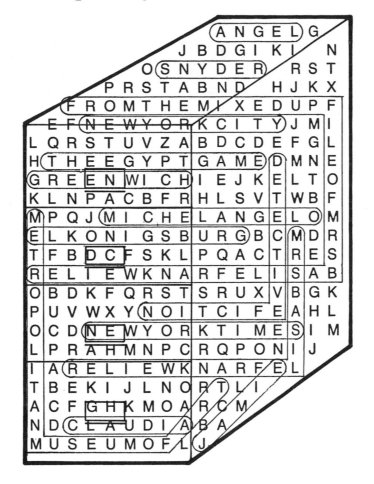

I—48 *The High King*

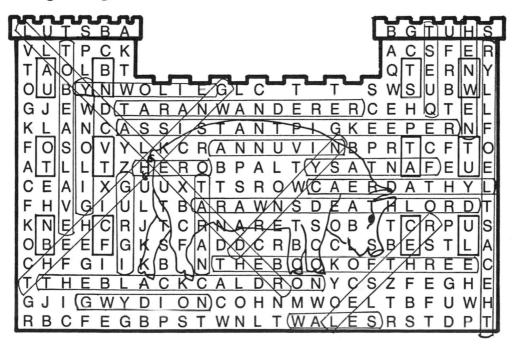

I–49 Sounder

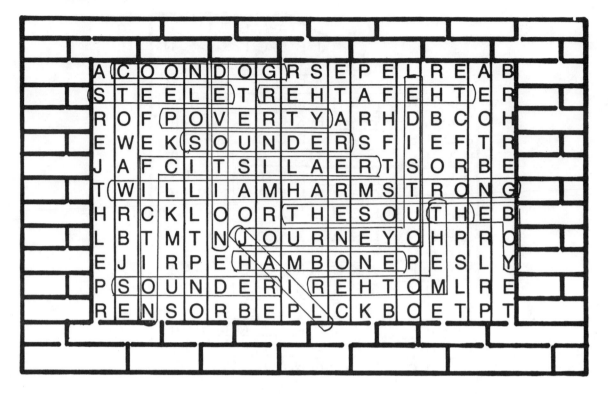

I–50 Summer of the Swans

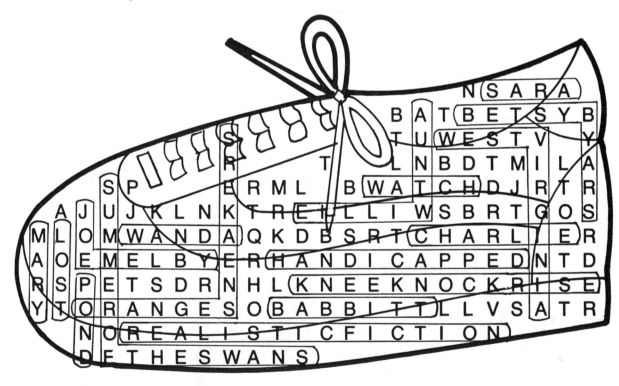

I–51 *Mrs. Frisby and the Rats of NIMH*

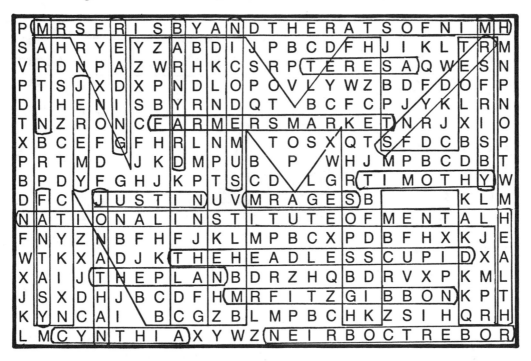

I–52 *Julie of the Wolves*

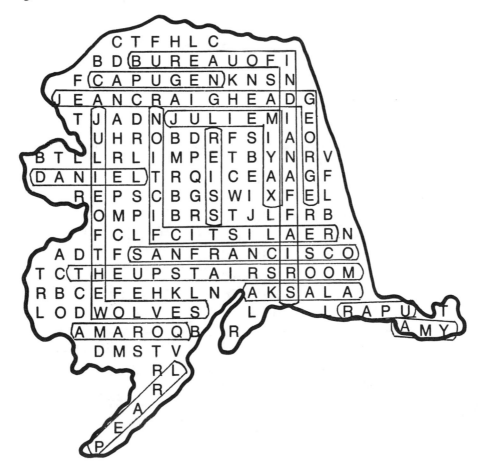

I-53 *The Slave Dancer*

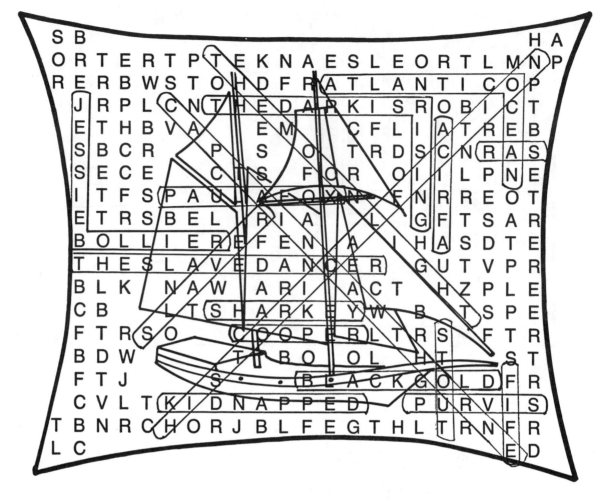

```
S B                                         H A
O R T E R T P T E K N A E S L E O R T L M N P
R E R B W S T O H D F R A T L A N T I C O P
  J R P L C N T H E D A R K I S R O B I C T
  E T H B V A   E M   C F L I A T R E B
  S B C R   P S O   T R D S C N R A S
  S E C E   C T S   F O R   O I L P N E
  I T F S P A U L A F O X N F N R R E O T
  E T R S B E L   R I A   L   G F S A R
  B O L L I E R E F E N A   I H A S D T E
  T H E S L A V E D A N C E R   G U T V P R
  B L K   N A W   A R I   A C T   H Z P L E R
  C B     L T S H A R K E Y W   B   T S P E R
  F T R S O   C O O P E R L T R S   T T R
  B D W       T   B O   O L     H T       S
  F T J     S . . B L A C K G O L D   F R
  C V L T K I D N A P P E D   P U R V I S
  T B N R C H O R J B L F E G T H L T R N F R
  L C                                     E D
```

I-54 *M. C. Higgins the Great*

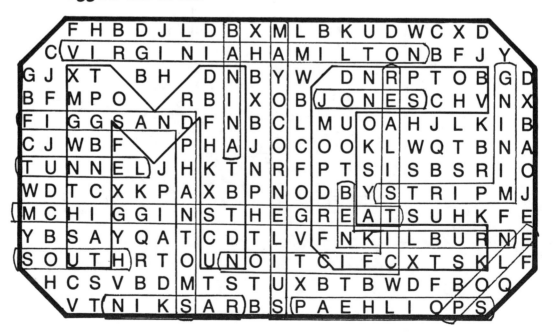

```
F H B D J L D B X M L B K U D W C X D
C V I R G I N I A H A M I L T O N B F J Y
G J X T   B H   D N B Y W   D N R P T O B G D
B F M P O     R B I N X O B J O N E S C H V N X
F I G G S A N D F N B   C L M U O A H J L K I B
C J W B F   P H A J O C O O K L W Q T B N A
T U N N E L J H K T N R F P T S I S B S R I O
W D T C X K P A X B P N O D B Y S T R I P M J
M C H I G G I N S T H E G R E A T S U H K F E
Y B S A Y Q A T C D T L V F N K I L B U R N E
S O U T H R T O U N O I T C I F C X T S K L F
  H C S V B D M T S T U X B T B W D F B O Q
  V T N I K S A R B S P A E H L I O P S
```

I–55 The Grey King

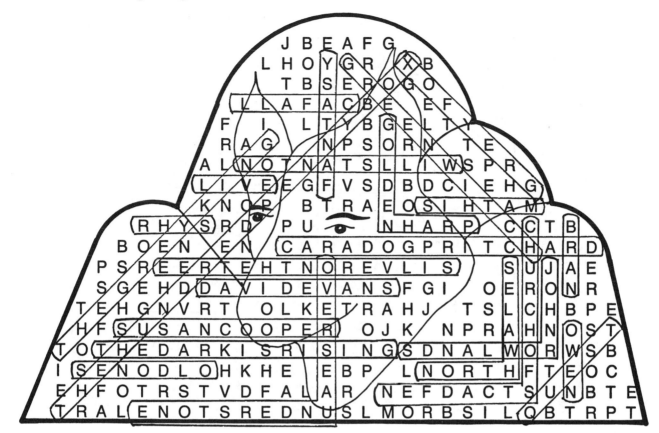

I–56 Roll of Thunder, Hear My Cry

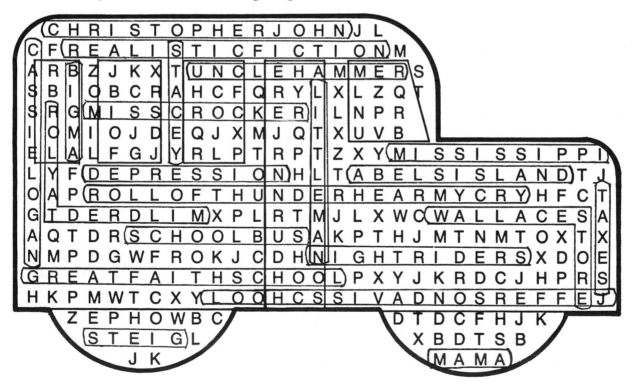

I–57 Bridge to Terabithia

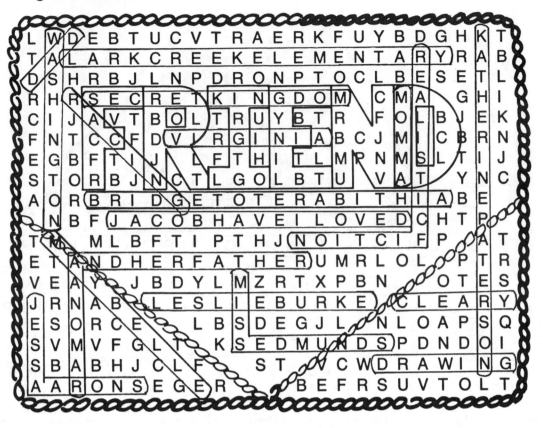

I–58 The Westing Game

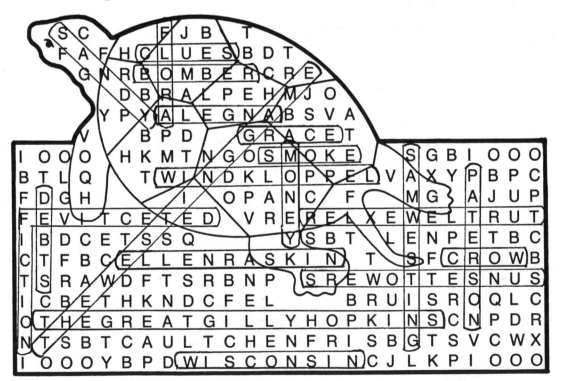

I–59 A Gathering of Days

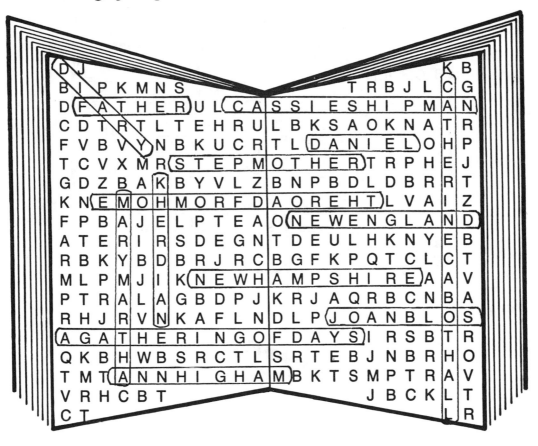

I–60 Jacob Have I Loved

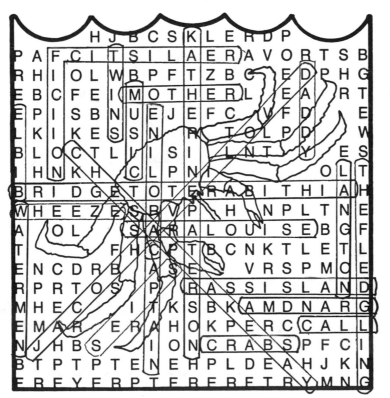

I–61 *A Visit to William Blake's Inn*

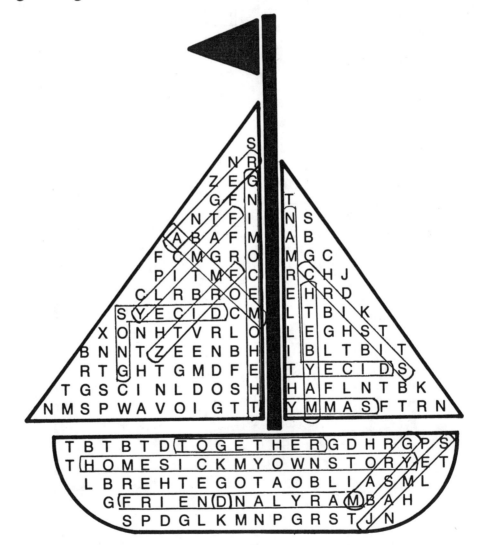

I–62 *Dicey's Song*

I–63 Dear Mr. Henshaw

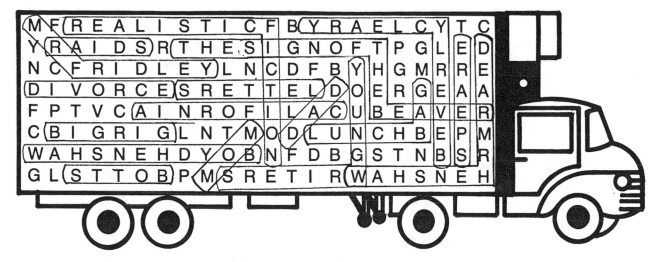

I–64 The Hero and the Crown

I-65 Sarah, Plain and Tall

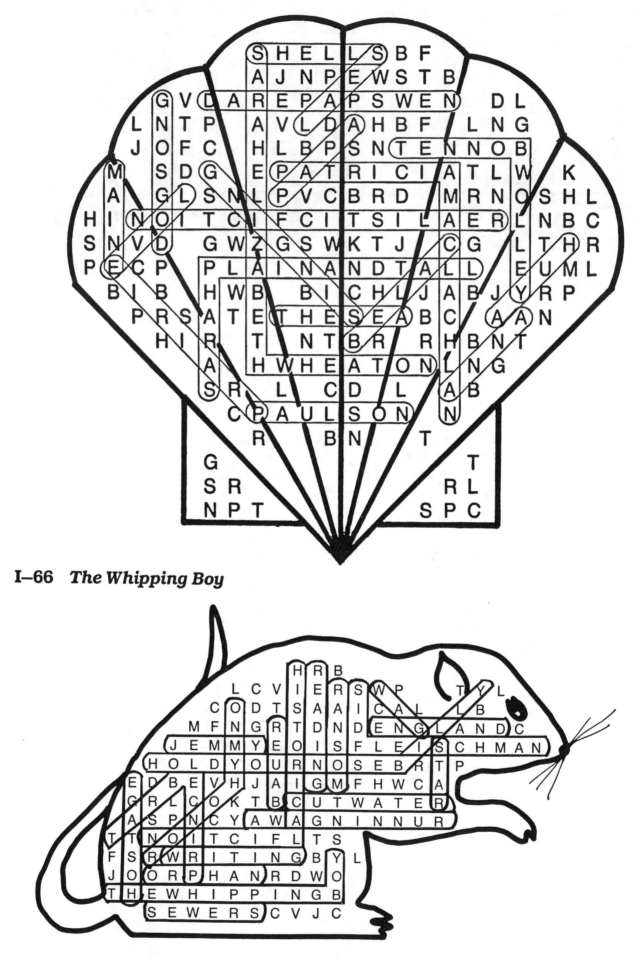

I-66 The Whipping Boy

I—67 *Lincoln: A Photobiography*

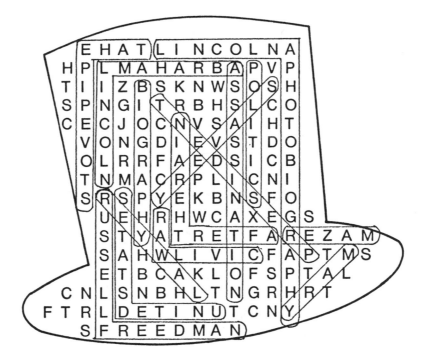

I—68 *Joyful Noise: Poems for Two Voices*

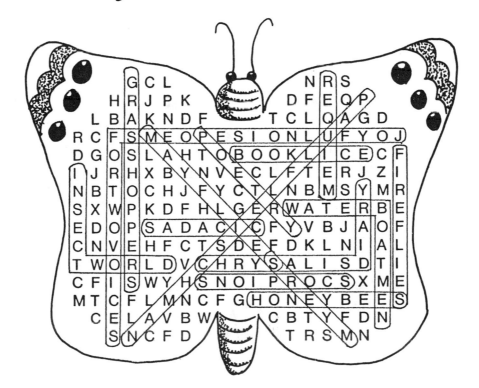

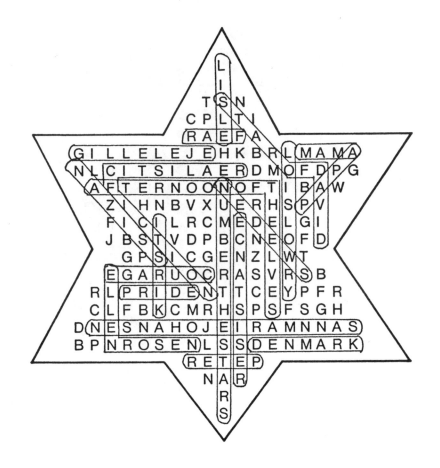

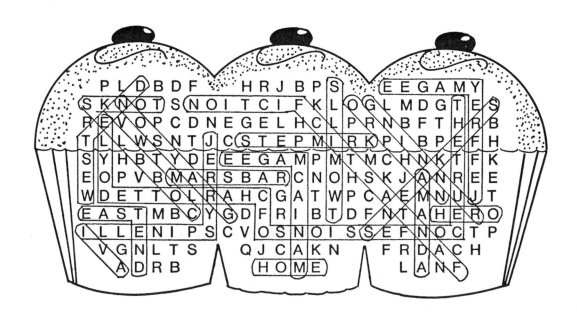

I–71 Shiloh

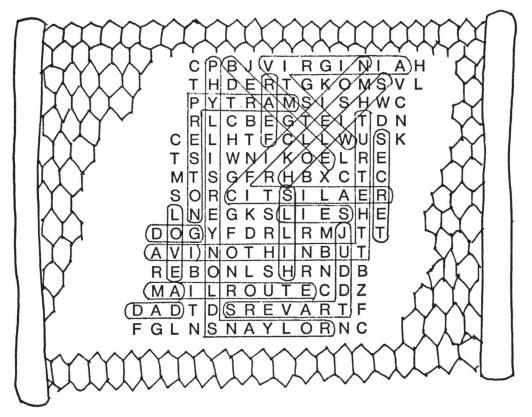

I–72 Missing May

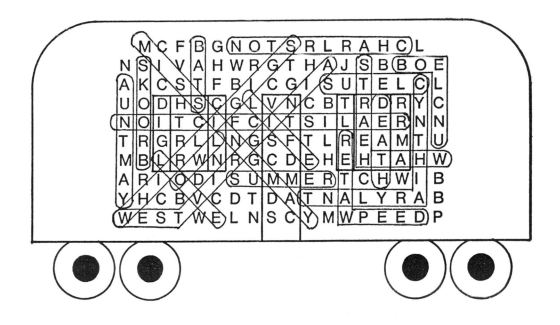

SECTION II: CALDECOTT AWARD ANSWER KEY

II–1 Animals of the Bible

II–2 Mei Li

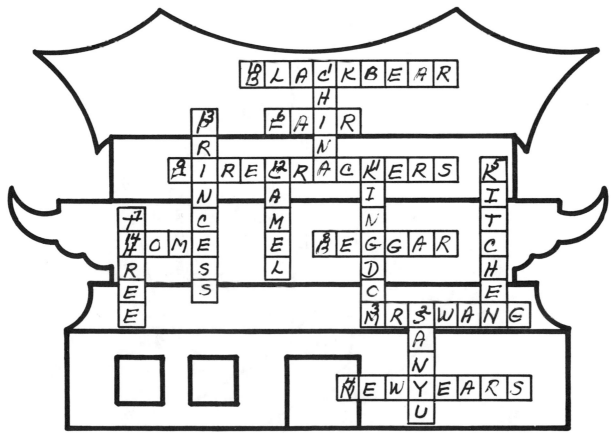

II–3 Abraham Lincoln

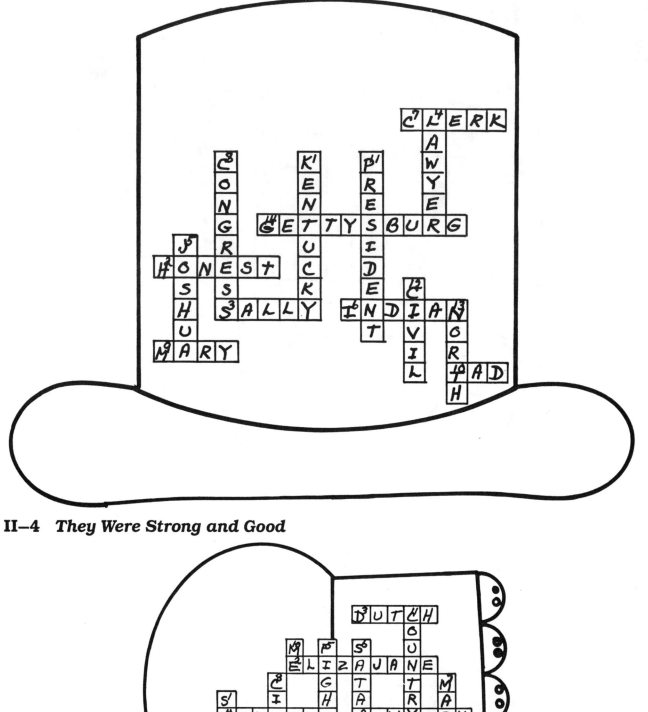

II–4 They Were Strong and Good

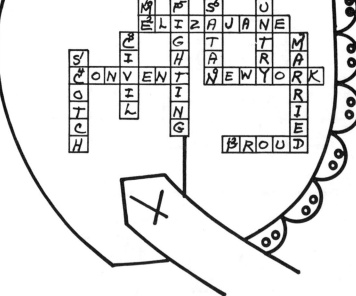

II–5 *Make Way for Ducklings*

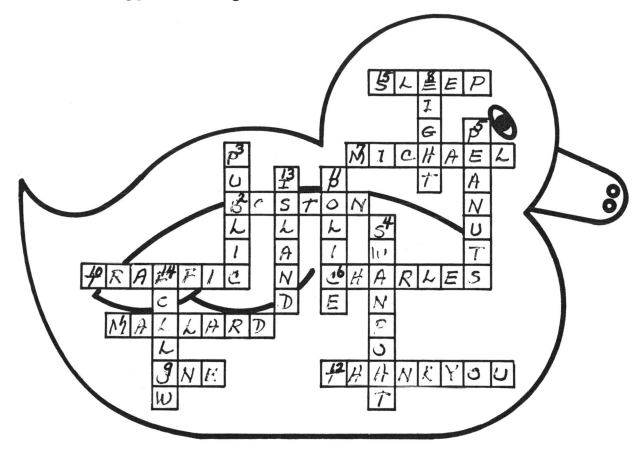

II–6 *The Little House*

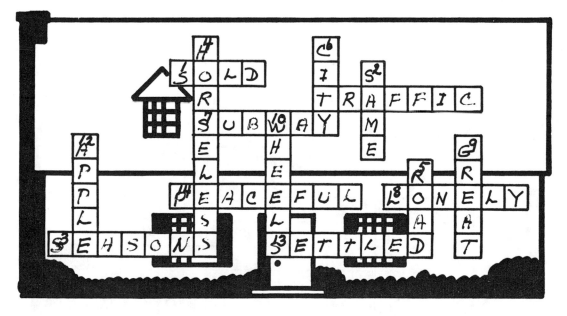

II–7 Many Moons

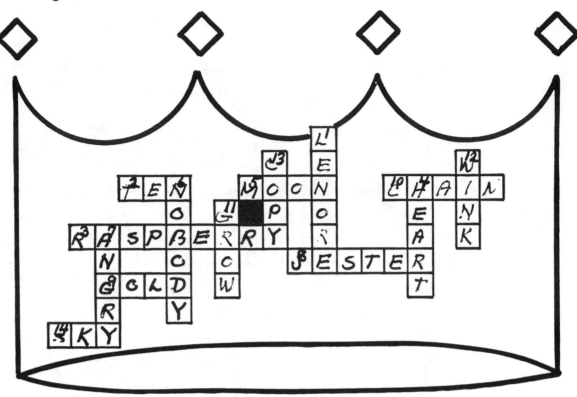

II–8 Prayer for a Child

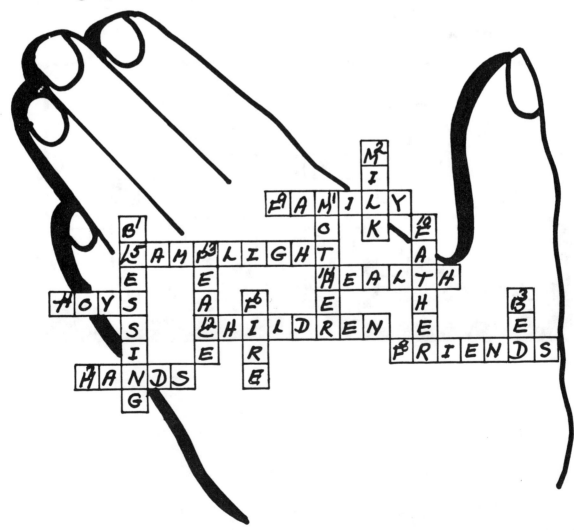

II–9 The Rooster Crows

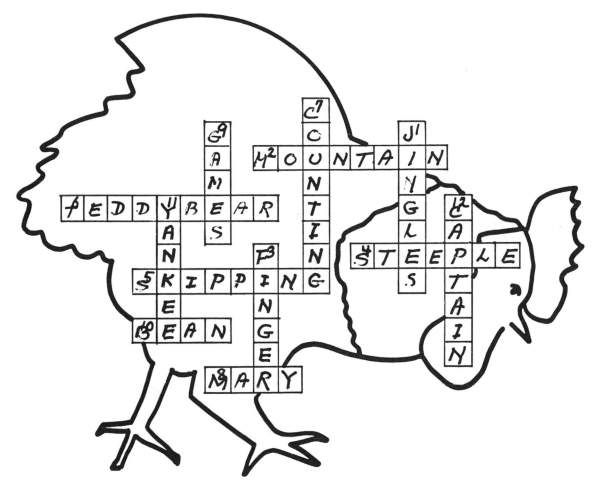

II–10 The Little Island

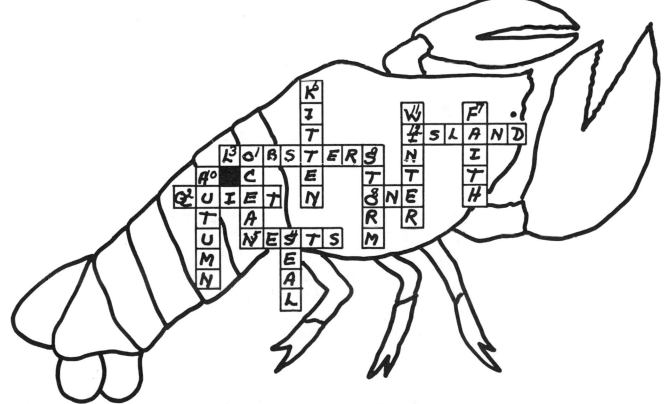

II–11 White Snow, Bright Snow

II–12 The Big Snow

II–13 Song of the Swallows

II–14 The Egg Tree

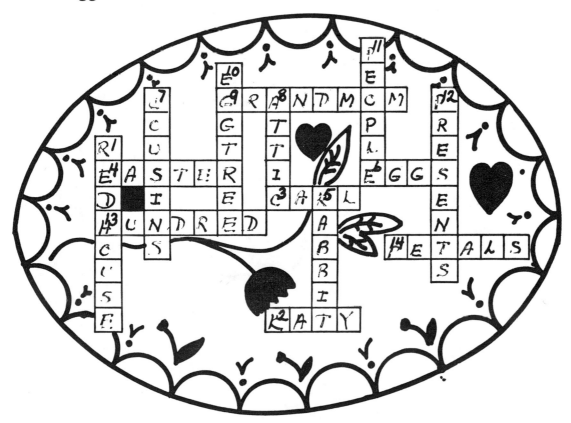

II–15 Finders Keepers

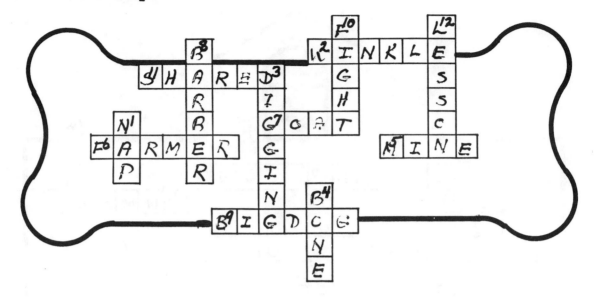

II–16 The Biggest Bear

II–17 Madeline's Rescue

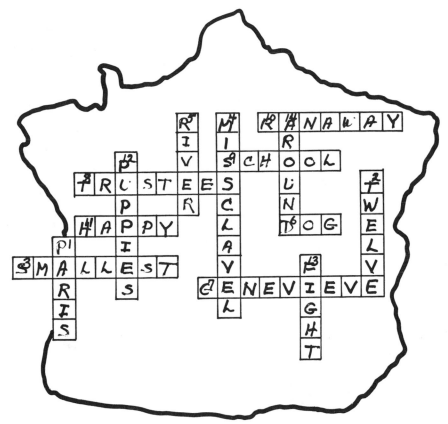

II–18 Cinderella

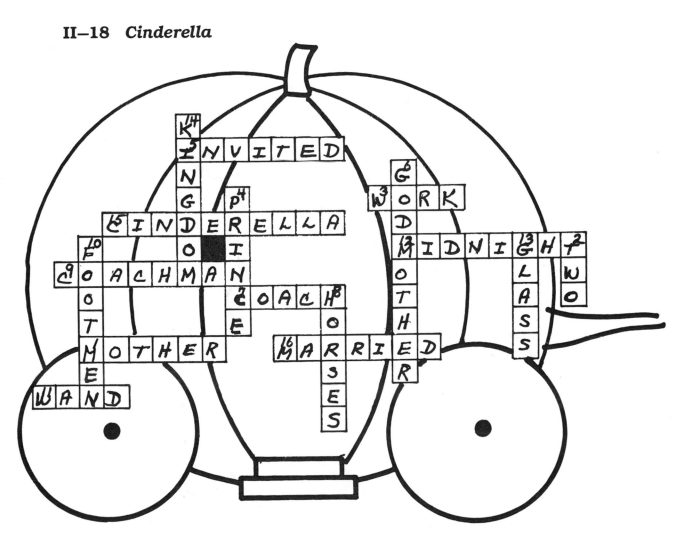

II—19 *Frog Went A-Courtin'*

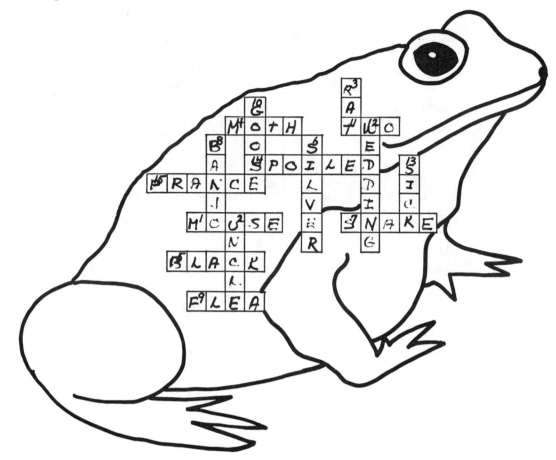

II—20 *A Tree Is Nice*

II–21 *Time of Wonder*

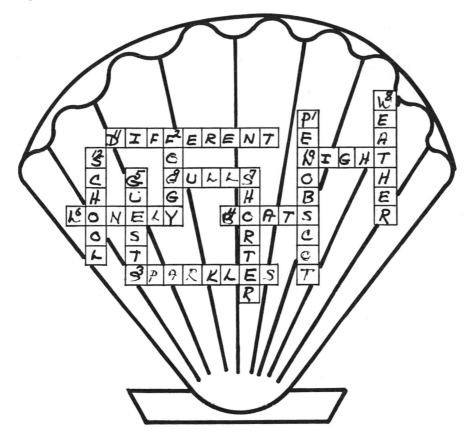

II–22 **Chanticleer and the Fox**

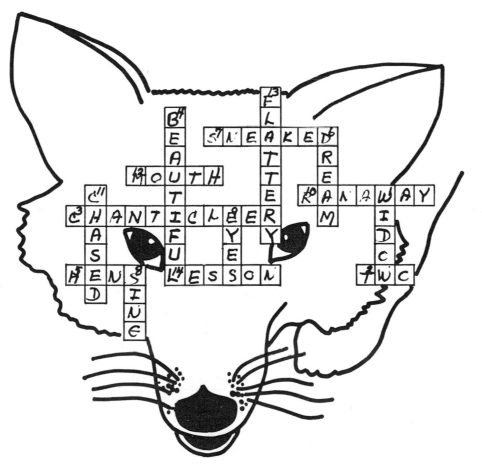

II—23 Nine Days to Christmas

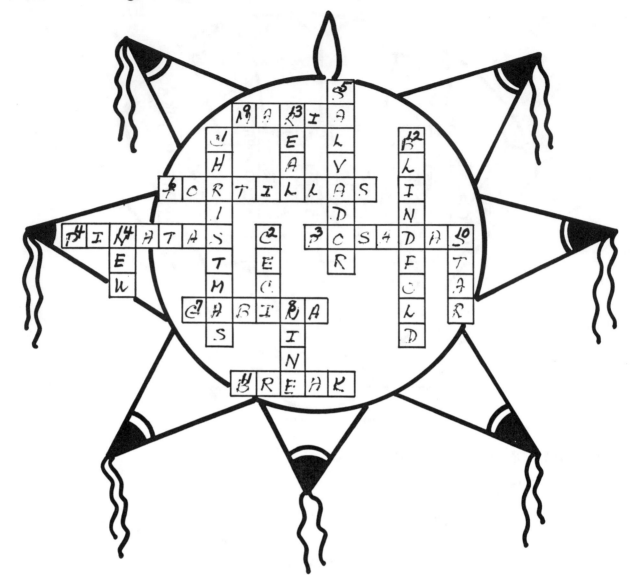

II—24 Baboushka and the Three Kings

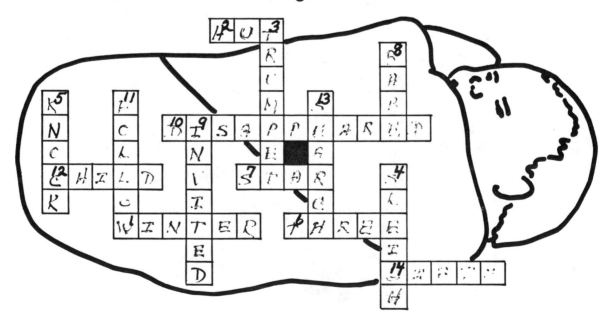

II—25 Once a Mouse...

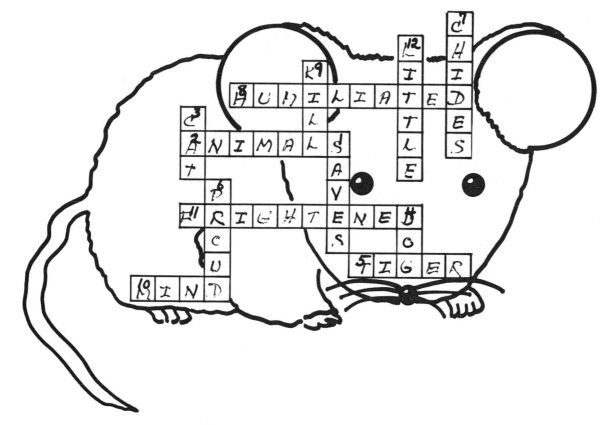

II—26 The Snowy Day

II—27 Where the Wild Things Are

II—28 May I Bring a Friend?

II—29 Always Room for One More

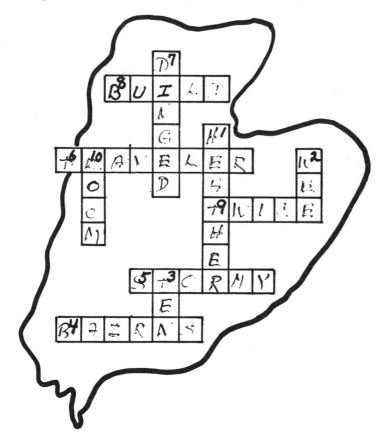

II—30 Sam, Bangs and Moonshine

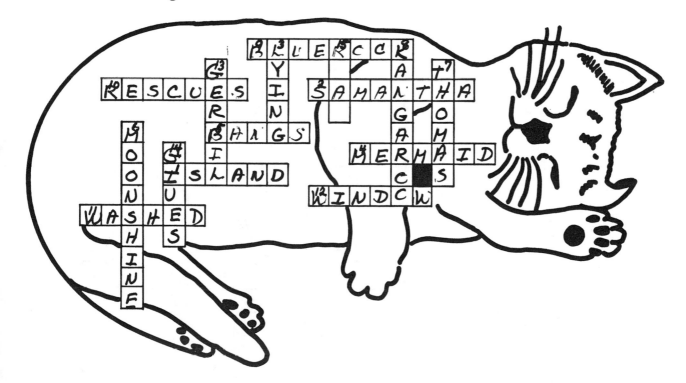

II–31 Drummer Hoff

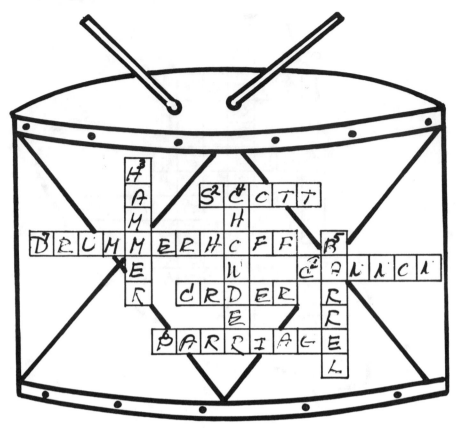

II–32 The Fool of the World and the Flying Ship

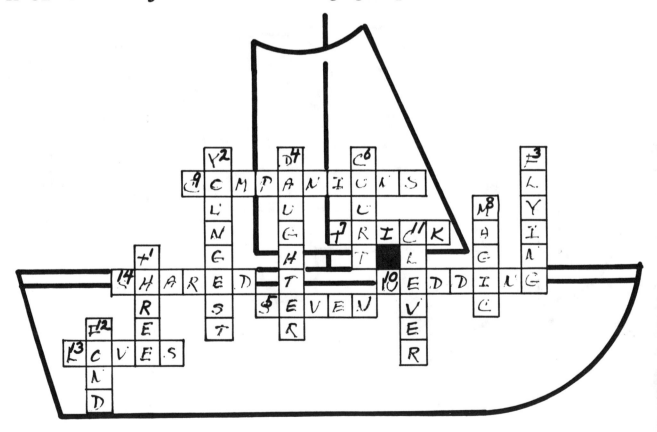

II—33 Sylvester and the Magic Pebble

II—34 A Story, A Story

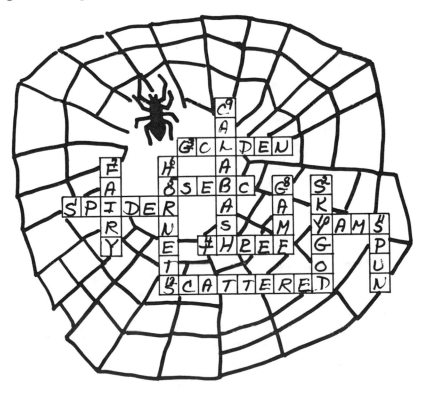

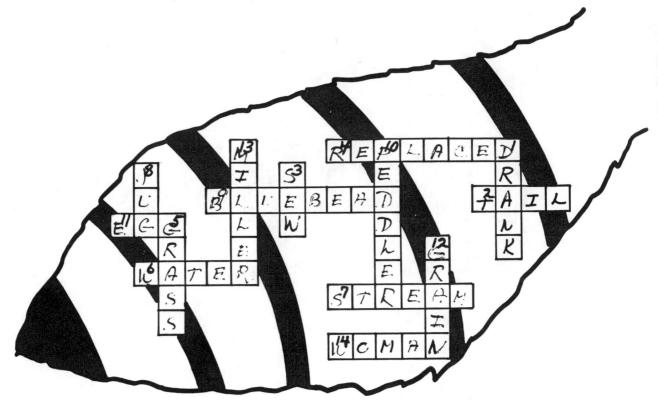

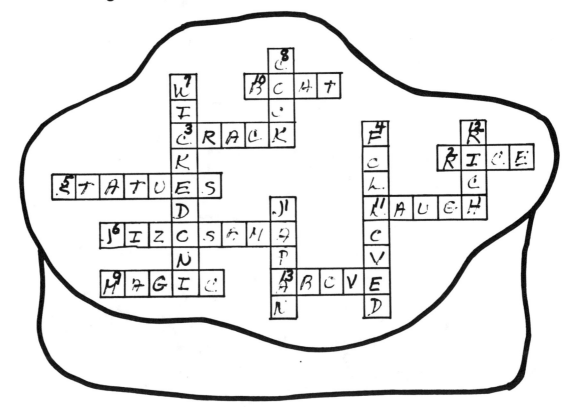

II–37 Duffy and the Devil

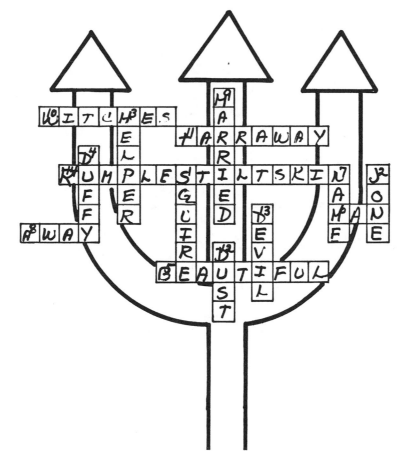

II–38 Arrow to the Sun

II–39 Why Mosquitoes Buzz in People's Ears

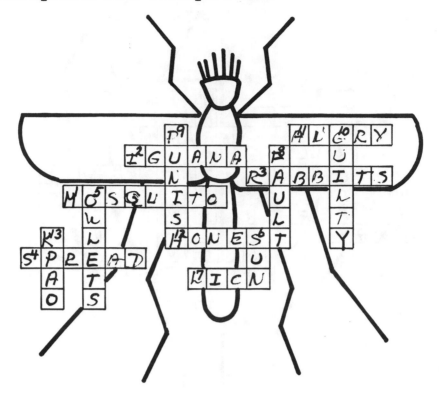

II–40 Ashanti to Zulu

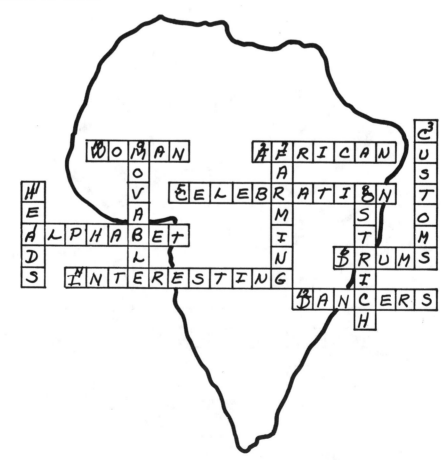

II–41 Noah's Ark

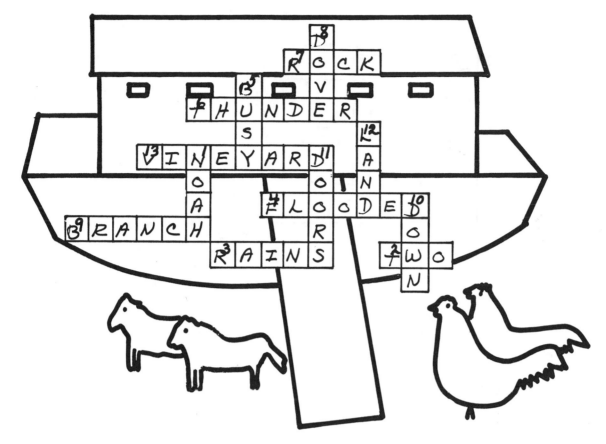

II–42 The Girl Who Loved Wild Horses

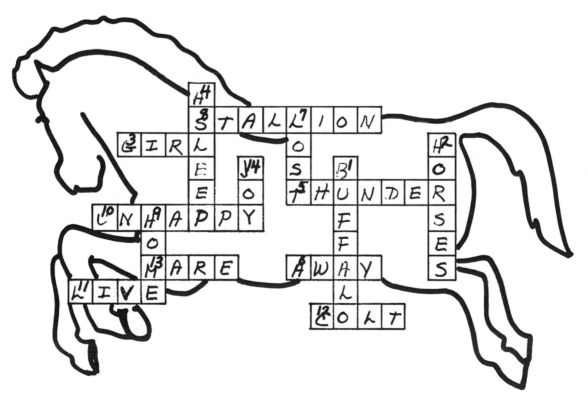

II—43 Ox-Cart Man

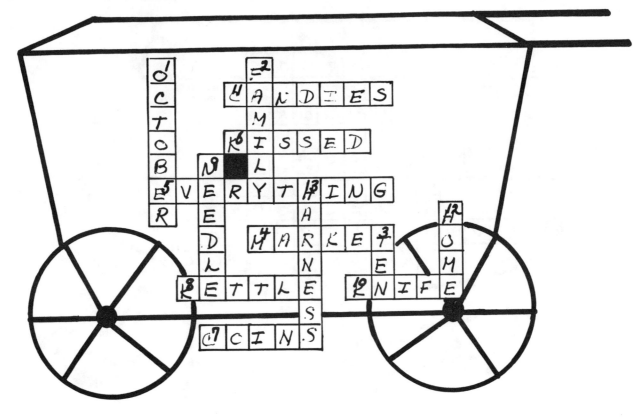

II—44 Fables

II—45 Jumanji

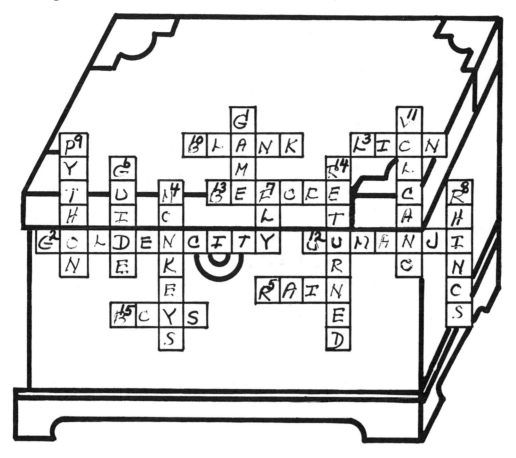

II—46 Shadow

II—47 The Glorious Flight

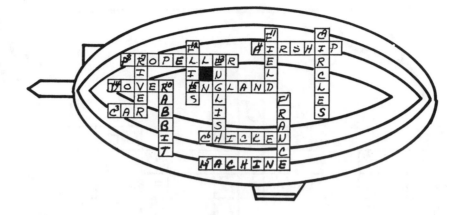

II—48 Saint George and the Dragon

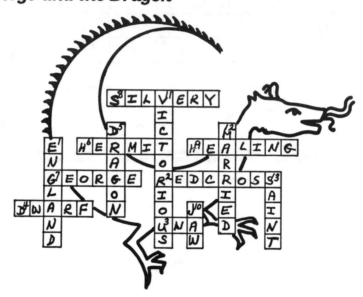

II-49 The Polar Express

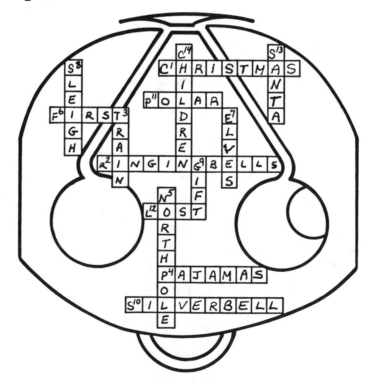

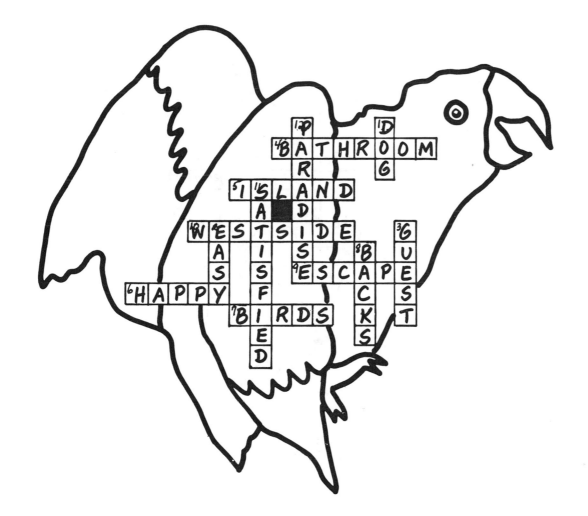

II–51 Owl Moon

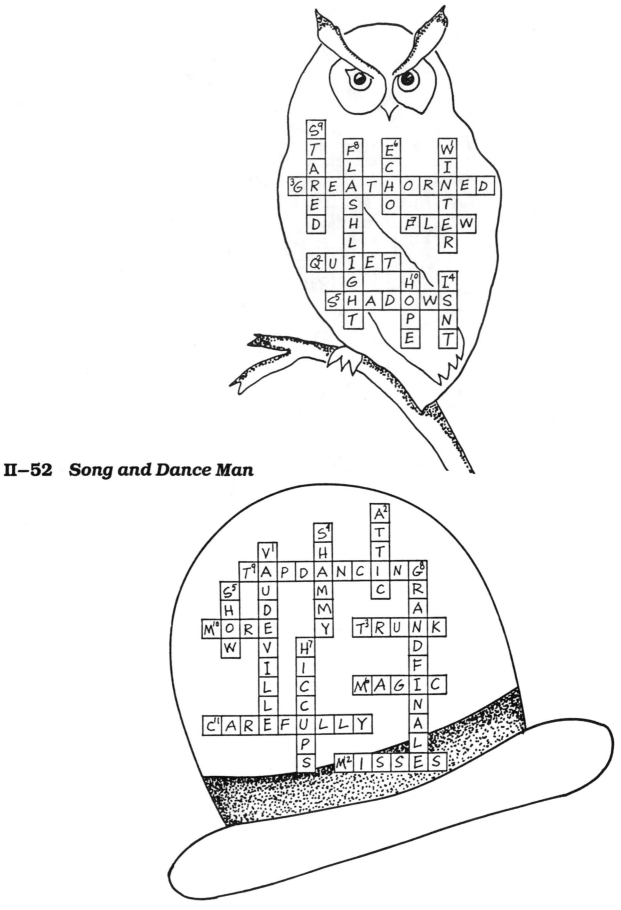

II–52 Song and Dance Man

II—53 *Lon Po Po*

II—54 *Black and White*

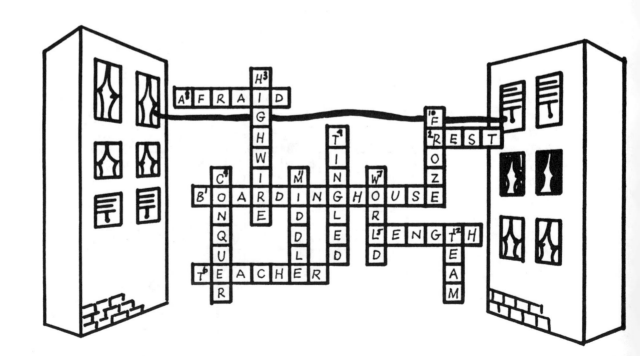

BIBLIOGRAPHY OF NEWBERY GOLD MEDAL BOOKS

(1922)   Van Loon, Hendrik Willem. *The Story of Mankind,* illustrated by the author. New York: Boni & Liveright, 1921. 548 pages. Historical nonfiction. *The history of man from prehistoric times until 1921.*

(1923)   Lofting, Hugh. *The Voyages of Doctor Dolittle,* illustrated by the author. New York: Frederick A. Stokes, 1922. 364 pages. Fantasy. *Written from the viewpoint of his assistant, Tommy Stubbins, the second book in a series about a naturalist who understands the languages of the animals.*

(1924)   Hawes, Charles B. *The Dark Frigate,* illustrated by Anton Otto Fischer. Boston: Atlantic Monthly, 1923. 247 pages. Historical fiction. *An experienced sailor at nineteen, Philip Marsham signs to sail on the Rose of Devon, which is captured by pirates.*

(1925)   Finger, Charles. *Tales from Silver Lands,* illustrated by Paul Honoré. Garden City, New York: Doubleday, Page, 1924. 207 pages. Folk tales. *Thirteen original folk tales of people and animals set throughout South America.*

(1926)   Crisman, Arthur Bowie. *Shen of the Sea,* illustrated by Else Hasselriis. New York: E. P. Dutton, 1925. 252 pages. Fantasy. *Sixteen short stories of Chinese people blending fantasy with realism.*

(1927)   James, Will. *Smoky the Cowhorse,* illustrated by the author. New York: Charles Scribner's Sons, 1926. 310 pages. Animal fiction. *The world of the American west as seen through the eyes of a horse.*

(1928)   Mukerji, Dhan Gopal. *Gay-Neck, The Story of a Pigeon,* illustrated by Boris Artzybasheff. New York: E. P. Dutton, 1927. 197 pages Realistic fiction. *The experiences of a carrier pigeon beginning in Calcutta before the First World War until its return to Calcutta after the war.*

(1929)   Kelly, Eric P. *The Trumpeter of Krakow,* illustrated by Angela Pruszynska. New York: Macmillan, 1928. 218 pages. Historical fiction. *How an act of bravery and self-sacrifice in ancient Krakow, Poland, saved a family two centuries later.*

(1930)   Field, Rachel. *Hitty, Her First Hundred Years,* illustrated by Dorothy Lathrop. New York: Macmillan, 1929. 207 pages. Fantasy. *The first-person account of a doll, including where and with whom she lived, during one hundred years.*

(1931)   Coatsworth, Elizabeth. *The Cat Who Went to Heaven,* illustrated by Lynd Ward. New York: Macmillan, 1930. 63 pages. Folk tale. *A small tricolored cat brings joy into the home of an artist and is finally blessed by Buddha.*

(1932)   Armer, Laura Adams. *Waterless Mountain,* illustrated by Sidney Armer. New York: Longmans, Green, 1931. 212 pages. Historical fiction. *Younger Brother, learning to become a medicine man, studies and reflects upon the customs of his people, the Navajo Indians.*

(1933)   Lewis, Elizabeth Foreman. *Young Fu of the Upper Yangtze,* illustrated by Kurt Wiese. Philadelphia: John C. Winston, 1932. 265 pages. Historical fiction. *Young Fu and his widowed mother live in Chungking, where he has the opportunity to be an apprentice to a master coppersmith.*

(1934) Meigs, Cornelia. *Invincible Louisa*. Boston: Little, Brown, 1933. 246 pages. Biography. *The nonfictional account of the life of Louisa May Alcott, the author of* **Little Women.**

(1935) Shannon, Monica. *Dobry,* illustrated by Atanas Katchmakoff. New York: Viking, 1934 (out of print). 176 pages. Foreign fiction. *Dobry, son of a Bulgarian peasant, wishes to become a sculptor rather than continue the family tradition of farming. Grandfather helps Dobry's mother to understand and support this ambition.*

(1936) Brink, Carol Ryrie. *Caddie Woodlawn,* illustrated by Kate Seredy. New York: Macmillan, 1935. 270 pages. Historical fiction. *The life of a frontier family in Wisconsin in 1864.*

(1937) Sawyer, Ruth. *Roller Skates,* illustrated by Valenti Angelo. New York: Viking, 1936. 186 pages. Historical fiction. *A year in the life of Lucinda and the unusual friends she meets when she lives in a boarding house while her parents are abroad.*

(1938) Seredy, Kate. *The White Stag,* illustrated by the author. New York: Viking, 1937. 95 pages. Folk tale. *The legendary story of the Huns and Magyars, their migration from Asia to Europe and their dream of finding a permanent home.*

(1939) Enright, Elizabeth. *Thimble Summer,* illustrated by the author. New York: Rinehart, 1938. 124 pages. Contemporary fiction. *One special summer in the life of Garnet Linden, a Wisconsin farm girl.*

(1940) Daugherty, James. *Daniel Boone,* illustrated by the author. New York: Viking, 1939 (out of print). 95 pages. Biography. *The life of the famous trailblazer set in an accurate portrayal of pioneer life.*

(1941) Sperry, Armstrong. *Call It Courage,* illustrated by the author. New York: Macmillan, 1940. 95 pages. Realistic fiction. *Mafatu, the chief's son, who has feared the sea since early childhood, sets off with only a dog and a bird to conquer that fear.*

(1942) Edmonds, Walter. *The Matchlock Gun,* illustrated by Paul Lantz. New York: Dodd, Mead, 1941. 50 pages. Historical fiction. *An old Dutch story of an occurrence during the French and Indian War in the small town of Guilderland outside of Albany, New York.*

(1943) Gray, Elizabeth Janet. *Adam of the Road,* illustrated by Robert Lawson. New York: Viking, 1942. 317 pages. Historical fiction. *A 13th-century English boy becomes separated from his father during a chase, so he sets out on foot to find him.*

(1944) Forbes, Esther. *Johnny Tremain,* illustrated by Lynd Ward. Boston: Houghton Mifflin, 1943. 256 pages. Historical fiction. *The story of a young Boston apprentice and the events leading up to the Revolutionary War.*

(1945) Lawson, Robert. *Rabbit Hill,* illustrated by the author. New York: Viking, 1944. 127 pages. Fantasy. *Georgie and the other animals on Rabbit Hill are excited but apprehensive when they learn "new folks" are moving into the "big house."*

(1946) Lenski, Lois. *Strawberry Girl,* illustrated by the author. Philadelphia: J. B. Lippincott, 1945. 193 pages. Historical fiction. *Birdie Boyer and her family attempt to homestead among the Florida "crackers" who do not accept "strangers" easily.*

(1947) Bailey, Carolyn Sherwin. *Miss Hickory,* illustrated by Ruth Gannett. New York: Viking, 1946. 123 pages. Fantasy. *Miss Hickory, a hickory nut and apple twig doll, must survive the winter left alone outdoors.*

(1948) Du Bois, William Pène. *The Twenty-One Balloons*, illustrated by the author. New York: Viking, 1947. 180 pages. Fantasy. *The fantastic adventures of Professor Sherman when his balloon lands on a volcanic island in the Pacific Ocean.*

(1949) Henry, Marguerite. *King of the Wind*, illustrated by Wesley Dennis. Chicago: Rand McNally, 1948. 175 pages. Realistic fiction. *The story of Sham, an Arabian stallion, who became one of the most famous horses of all time, the Godolphin Arabian.*

(1950) De Angeli, Marguerite. *The Door in the Wall*, illustrated by the author. Garden City, New York: Doubleday, 1949. 121 pages. Historical fiction. *Robin, the son of a great English lord, overcomes his disabilities and wins knighthood.*

(1951) Yates, Elizabeth. *Amos Fortune, Free Man*, illustrated by Nora Unwin. New York: Alladin, 1950, 181 pages. Biography. *The son of an African king who is brought to the United States as a slave and eventually wins his freedom.*

(1952) Estes, Eleanor. *Ginger Pye*, illustrated by the author. New York: Harcourt, Brace, 1951. 250 pages. Family fiction. *Jerry and Rachel dearly love their dog Ginger. Are the appearance of the man with the mustard-colored hat and the disappearance of Ginger connected?*

(1953) Clark, Ann Nolan. *Secret of the Andes*, illustrated by Jean Charlot. New York: Viking, 1952. 130 pages. Foreign fiction. *Cusi, the Inca Indian boy, lives high in the Andes guarding the llama flock and learning to take his rightful place with his people.*

(1954) Krumgold, Joseph. *And Now Miguel*, illustrated by Jean Charlot. New York: Thomas Y. Crowell, 1953. 245 pages. Realistic fiction. *Miguel's secret wish is to go with the men to the Sangre de Cristo Mountains in New Mexico when they take the sheep to summer pasture.*

(1955) De Jong, Meindert. *The Wheel on the School*, illustrated by Maurice Sendak. New York: Harper, 1954. 298 pages. Foreign fiction. *Lina and the other schoolchildren need a wheel to place on the roof of the schoolhouse to bring the storks back to Shora, a small town on the North Sea in the Netherlands.*

(1956) Latham, Jean Lee. *Carry On, Mr. Bowditch*, illustrated by John O'Hara Cosgrave. Boston: Houghton Mifflin, 1955. 251 pages. Biography. *The life of Nathaniel Bowditch, who became an expert in ship navigation. His book, New American Practical Navigator, set the standards for navigation.*

(1957) Sorensen, Virginia. *Miracles on Maple Hill*, illustrated by Beth and Joe Krush. New York: Harcourt, Brace, 1956. 180 pages. Realistic fiction. *Marly's father returns from the Second World War having to readjust after being a prisoner-of-war. She hopes the family's move to a farm will bring the family back together.*

(1958) Keith, Harold, *Rifles for Watie*. New York: Thomas Y. Crowell, 1957. 332 pages. Historical fiction. *Jeff Bussey of Kansas joins the Union volunteers during the Civil War, never dreaming he would become an espionage agent as well as a soldier.*

(1959) Speare, Elizabeth George. *The Witch of Blackbird Pond*. Boston: Houghton Mifflin, 1958. 249 pages. Historical fiction. *Visiting her aunt in Connecticut in the 1600s, Kit Tyler is branded a witch due to her association with a woman already branded a witch.*

(1960) Krumgold, Joseph. *Onion John*, illustrated by Symeon Shimin. New York: Thomas Y. Crowell, 1959. 248 pages. Realistic fiction. *The unusual but warm friendship of 12-year-old Andy Rusch and Onion John, the town's "odd-jobs" man.*

(1961)   O'Dell, Scott. *Island of the Blue Dolphins*. Boston: Houghton Mifflin, 1960. 184 pages. Historical fiction. *The historical first-person account of Karana, the lone survivor of the kidnapping of her people from the island of San Nicolas and her 18 years of solitary life on the island.*

(1962)   Speare, Elizabeth George. *The Bronze Bow*. Boston: Houghton Mifflin, 1961. 255 pages. Historical fiction. *The story of Daniel Bar Jamin, who for personal revenge and patriotism, fights to rid his land of the Roman legions. This hatred affects his friendships and relationships with those close to him.*

(1963)   L'Engle, Madeleine. *A Wrinkle in Time*. New York: Farrar, Straus, 1962. 211 pages. Science fiction. *Meg Murry, Charles Wallace, and Calvin search for Meg's and Charles' fathers, who are missing while on a secret mission for the government.*

(1964)   Neville, Emily. *It's Like This, Cat*, illustrated by Emil Weiss. New York: Harper & Row, 1963. 180 pages. Realistic fiction. *The first-person account of Dave Mitchell, the cat he befriends, and his problems with family and friends.*

(1965)   Wojciechowska, Maia. *Shadow of a Bull*, illustrated by Alvin Smith. New York: Atheneum, 1964. 165 pages. Foreign fiction. *Being the son of a great bullfighter, Manolo is expected to carry on his dead father's tradition. Conflict arises as Manolo wants to be a doctor, not a bullfighter.*

(1966)   De Trevino, Elizabeth Borton. *I, Juan de Pareja*. New York: Farrar, Straus & Giroux, 1965. 180 pages. Biography. *The 17th-century story set in Spain of Juan de Pareja who, although a slave, became an accomplished and respected artist under the tutorage of Diego Velázquez.*

(1967)   Hunt, Irene. *Up a Road Slowly*. Chicago: Follett, 1966. 192 pages. Realistic fiction. *After the death of her mother, Julie is sent to live with her maiden aunt. Julie slowly learns the values her aunt lives by and finally understands the importance of integrity, compassion, and strength of character.*

(1968)   Konigsburg, Elaine. *From the Mixed-Up Files of Mrs. Basil E. Frankweiler*, illustrated by the author. New York: Atheneum, 1967. 162 pages. Contemporary fiction. *Claudia, feeling bored and unappreciated, plans to run away. She chooses Jamie, her younger brother, to go with her and selects the Metropolitan Museum of Art as the place to run away to.*

(1969)   Alexander, Lloyd. *The High King*. New York: Holt, Rinehart & Winston, 1968. 285 pages. Fantasy. *The fifth and final volume of the Chronicles of Prydain, this is the quest of Taran to recover the most powerful weapon in Prydain from the baron who wants to destroy the kingdom.*

(1970)   Armstrong, William. *Sounder*, illustrated by James Barkley. New York: Harper & Row, 1969. 116 pages. Realistic fiction. *The great coon dog, Sounder, has a great loyalty to the black sharecropper and his family. But not even Sounder can save his master when hunger drives the man to steal food.*

(1971)   Byars, Betsy. *Summer of the Swans*, illustrated by Ted CoConis. New York: Viking, 1970. 142 pages. Realistic fiction. *The realistic story of Sara and the problems she faces with her mentally retarded brother. His disappearance brings Sara a new understanding of life and a new friend.*

(1972)   O'Brien, Robert C. *Mrs. Frisby and the Rats of NIMH*, illustrated by Zena Bernstein. New York: Atheneum, 1971. 233 pages. Fantasy. *Mrs. Frisby, widow of*

Jonathan Frisby, must move her ill son, Timothy, from their winter home to their summer home. She receives help from a group of highly trained rats who have escaped from the National Institute of Mental Health.

(1973) George, Jean. *Julie of the Wolves*, illustrated by John Schoenherr. New York: Harper & Row, 1972. 170 pages. Realistic fiction. *Miyax, an Eskimo girl, runs away from an intolerable home situation. Lost and helpless on the North Slope in Alaska, the wolves save her life.*

(1974) Fox, Paula. *The Slave Dancer*, illustrated by Eros Keith. Scarsdale, New York: Bradbury, 1973. 176 pages. Historical fiction. *Jessie Bollier is kidnapped and taken aboard The Moonlight, a slave ship bound for West Africa.*

(1975) Hamilton, Virginia. *M. C. Higgins the Great.* New York: Macmillan, 1974. 278 pages. Realistic fiction. *High at the top of a 40-foot pole, Mayo Cornelius Higgins dreams of escaping the narrow confines closing in his family.*

(1976) Cooper, Susan. *The Grey King*, illustrated by Michael Heslop. New York: Atheneum, 1975. 208 pages. Fantasy. *The fourth in **The Dark Is Rising** series, Will Stanton arrives in North Wales to sound the golden harp and awaken the six sleepers.*

(1977) Taylor, Mildred D. *Roll of Thunder, Hear My Cry*, frontispiece by Jerry Pinkney. New York: Dial, 1976. 276 pages. Realistic fiction. *The story of Cassie Logan and her family during the days of the Depression when black people faced seemingly insurmountable problems.*

(1978) Paterson, Katherine. *The Bridge to Terabithia*, illustrated by Donna Diamond. New York: Thomas Y. Crowell, 1977. 128 pages. Realistic fiction. *Jess Aarons has never before met anyone like Leslie Burke, a new neighbor. She comes into his life and changes everything, then leaves him to sort out the problems alone.*

(1979) Raskin, Ellen. *The Westing Game.* New York: E. P. Dutton, 1978. 185 pages. Mystery fiction. *Turtle Wexler is involved as one of 16 people invited to the reading of Sam Westing's will. They are given a set of clues and a chance to become a millionaire if the mystery is solved.*

(1980) Blos, Joan. *A Gathering of Days: A New England Girl's Journal, 1830–1832.* New York: Charles Scribner's Sons, 1979. 144 pages. Historical fiction. *In diary format, two years in the life of Catherine Cabot Hall, 13 years old, of Meredith, New Hampshire.*

(1981) Paterson, Katherine. *Jacob Have I Loved.* New York: Thomas Y. Crowell, 1980. 216 pages. Historical fiction. *Being twins is not easy, especially when Louise feels Caroline is the one everyone prefers. Louise must fight to reach a sense of security which Caroline cannot disturb.*

(1982) Willard, Nancy. *A Visit to William Blake's Inn: Poems for Innocent and Experienced Travelers*, illustrated by Alice and Martin Provensen. New York: Harcourt Brace Jovanovich, 1981. 44 pages. Poetical fiction. *A collection of poems describing the unusual people and animals who are guests at the imaginary inn of William Blake.*

(1983) Voigt, Cynthia. *Dicey's Song.* New York: Atheneum, 1982. 196 pages. Realistic fiction. *In the sequel to **The Homecoming**, Dicey and her brothers and sister hope to secure a place in Grandmother's heart and become a family.*

(1984) Cleary, Beverly. *Dear Mr. Henshaw*, illustrated by Paul O. Zelinsky. New York: Morrow, 1983. 133 pages. Realistic fiction. *A series of letters from a boy to an author, pouring out his frustrating problems.*

(1985) McKinley, Robin. *The Hero and the Crown*. New York: Greenwillow Books, 1984. 246 pages. Fantasy. *Aerin, daughter of the king of Damar and a witchwoman of Damar, proves her destiny through fighting dragons. Finally she battles Agsded, the evil mage, to restore the Hero's Crown to Damar.*

(1986) MacLachlan, Patricia. *Sarah, Plain and Tall*. New York: Harper & Row, 1985. 64 pages. Realistic fiction. *Sarah comes from Maine to a pioneer family for a month's trial in response to a newspaper ad for a wife and mother.*

(1987) Fleischman, Sid. *The Whipping Boy*. New York: Greenwillow Books, 1986, 90 pages. Historical fiction. *Jemmy, an orphan boy, serves as whipping boy to the heir of the throne. Jemmy's dream of running away, conflicts with Prince Brat's when the two find themselves involved in a suspence-filled adventure.*

(1988) Freedman, Russell. *Lincoln: A Photobiography*. New York: Clarion Books, 1987. 150 pages. Biography. *A fascinating, pictorial account of Abraham Lincoln including his boyhood, law career, and family, as well as his years as president of the United States.*

(1989) Fleischman, Paul. *Joyful Noise: Poems for Two Voices*. New York: Harper & Row, 1988. 44 pages. Poetic fiction. *An exuberant, pulsating, distinctive collection of verses from the insect world.*

(1990) Lowry, Lois. *Number the Stars*. Boston: Houghton Mifflin Company, 1989. 139 pages. Historical fiction. *In spite of great danger to themselves, Annmarie Johansen and her family shelter Ellen Rosen during the Nazi occupation of Denmark.*

(1991) Spinelli, Jerry. *Maniac Magee*. Boston: Little, Brown and Company, 1990. 184 pages. Realistic fiction. *Jeffrey Lionel Magee, homeless after the accidental death of his parents, becomes a living legend in the east side as well as the west side of town.*

(1992) Naylor, Phyllis Reynolds. *Shiloh*. New York: Atheneum, 1991. 144 pages. Realistic fiction. *Marty believes Judd Travers is abusing the beagle. He hides and cares for the dog, hoping to find a way to buy the dog from Judd.*

(1993) Rylant, Cynthia. *Missing May*. New York: Orchard Books, 1992. 89 pages. Realistic fiction. *Aunt May has died. Summer, with the help of Cletus, searches desperately for a way to give a new meaning of life to both Uncle Ob and herself.*

BIBLIOGRAPHY OF CALDECOTT GOLD MEDAL BOOKS

(1938) Fish, Helen Dean. *Animals of the Bible,* illustrated by Dorothy Lathrop. New York: Frederick A. Stokes, 1937. 66 pages. Religious nonfiction. *Bible verses emphasizing the animal world and introducing man.*

(1939) Handforth, Thomas. *Mei Li,* illustrated by the author. Garden City, New York: Doubleday, 1938. 48 pages. Holiday fiction. *A small Chinese girl has three pennies to spend at the New Year's fair in Peiping. After an eventful day, she arrives home in time to greet the Kitchen God at midnight.*

(1940) d'Aulaire, Ingri, and Edgar d'Aulaire. *Abraham Lincoln,* illustrated by the authors. Garden City, New York: Doubleday, 1939. 56 pages. Biography. *The life of Abraham Lincoln.*

(1941) Lawson, Robert. *They Were Strong and Good,* illustrated by the author. New York: Viking, 1940. 66 pages. Biography. *The story of Robert Lawson's parents and grandparents.*

(1942) McCloskey, Robert. *Make Way for Ducklings,* illustrated by the author. New York: Viking, 1941. 72 pages. Fantasy. *Mr. and Mrs. Mallard search Boston for the right place to build a nest, raise their eight ducklings, and settle down permanently.*

(1943) Burton, Virginia Lee. *The Little House,* illustrated by the author. Boston: Houghton Mifflin, 1942. 40 pages. Fantasy. *How a sturdy little house built in the country becomes surrounded by the city and returns to the country.*

(1944) Thurber, James. *Many Moons,* illustrated by Louis Slobodkin. New York: Harcourt, Brace, 1943. 48 pages. Fantasy. *Princess Lenore wants the moon. After all others fail, the court jester proves she can have the moon and also see it in the sky.*

(1945) Field, Rachel. *Prayer for a Child,* illustrated by Elizabeth Orton Jones. New York: Macmillan, 1944. 32 pages. Religious fiction. *The prayer of a small child giving thanks for what is important in her life.*

(1946) Petersham, Maud, and Miska Petersham. *The Rooster Crows,* illustrated by the authors. New York: Macmillan, 1945. 64 pages. Collection. *American rhymes and jingles.*

(1947) MacDonald, Golden. *The Little Island,* illustrated by Leonard Weisgard. Garden City, New York: Doubleday, 1946. 48 pages. Fantasy. *A small kitten discovers that the little island that seemed far away from the world is really a part of the world.*

(1948) Tresselt, Alvin. *White Snow, Bright Snow,* illustrated by Roger Duvoisin. New York: Lothrop, Lee & Shephard, 1947. 32 pages. Seasonal fiction. *The magic of the winter season—from the first snowflake to the last.*

(1949) Hader, Berta, and Elmer Hader. *The Big Snow,* illustrated by the authors. New York: Macmillan, 1948. 48 pages. Seasonal fiction. *How the animals cope during the long winter season.*

(1950) Politi, Leo. *Song of the Swallows,* illustrated by the author. New York: Charles Scribner's Sons, 1949. 32 pages. Seasonal fiction. *Juan, a small boy, and Julian, the old gardener and bell ringer, welcome the swallows on their annual return to the mission of San Juan Capistrano.*

(1951) Milhous, Katherine. *The Egg Tree,* illustrated by the author. New York: Charles Scribner's Sons, 1950. 32 pages. Holiday fiction. *With Grandmother's help, Katy and*

Carl and the other children make a decorated egg tree which friends and neighbors enjoy during the Easter season.

(1952) Lipkind, William. *Finders Keepers,* illustrated by Nicolas Mordvinoff. New York: Harcourt, Brace, 1951. 36 pages. Fantasy. *Two dogs, Nap and Winkle, almost lose a good bone because they cannot decide whose bone it should be.*

(1953) Ward, Lynd. *The Biggest Bear,* illustrated by the author. Boston: Houghton Mifflin, 1952. 85 pages. Realistic fiction. *Johnny's small bear cub presents problems as he grows until Johnny must get rid of the bear—but the bear won't go.*

(1954) Bemelmans, Ludwig. *Madeline's Rescue,* illustrated by the author. New York: Viking, 1953. 56 pages. Foreign fiction. *Madeline is rescued by a small dog who comes to live with Madeline and the other little girls in a Paris convent. The dog runs away, but returns with a present for all the girls.*

(1955) Perrault, Charles. *Cinderella,* translated and illustrated by Marcia Brown. New York: Charles Scribner's Sons, 1954. 32 pages. Folk tale. *Marcia Brown's version of the tale of Cinderella.*

(1956) Langstaff, John, ed. *Frog Went A-Courtin',* illustrated by Feodor Rojankovsky. New York: Harcourt, Brace, 1955. 32 pages. Mother Goose tale. *The ballad of Frog retold by John Langstaff and set to music and illustrated.*

(1957) Udry, Janice May. *A Tree Is Nice,* illustrated by Marc Simont. New York: Harper & Brothers, 1956. 32 pages. Science nonfiction. *The many reasons why having a tree enhances a child's life.*

(1958) McCloskey, Robert. *Time of Wonder,* illustrated by the author. New York: Viking, 1957. 64 pages. Seasonal fiction. *The beauty of the summer season on an island in Maine and the family that enjoys it.*

(1959) Chaucer, Geoffrey. *Chanticleer and the Fox,* translated by Robert Mayer Lumiansky. Adapted and illustrated by Barbara Cooney. New York: Thomas Y. Crowell, 1958. 36 pages. Folk tale. *A beautiful cock almost loses his life to a fox because of his foolish pride.*

(1960) Ets, Marie Hall, and Aurora Labastida. *Nine Days to Christmas,* illustrated by Marie Hall Ets. New York: Viking, 1959. 48 pages. Holiday fiction. *The preparation for the Christmas festival in Mexico, as seen through the eyes of small Ceci.*

(1961) Robbins, Ruth. *Baboushka and the Three Kings,* illustrated by Nicolas Sidjakov. Berkeley, California: Parnassus, 1960. 28 pages. Folk tale. *The old Russian tale of Baboushka and her endless search for the Christ child.*

(1962) Brown, Marcia. *Once a Mouse...,* illustrated by the author. New York: Charles Scribner's Sons, 1961. 32 pages. Folk tale. *An old tale from India of how a hermit transforms a mouse into a mighty tiger, but pride causes the mouse's downfall.*

(1963) Keats, Ezra Jack. *The Snowy Day,* illustrated by the author. New York: Viking, 1962. 32 pages. Seasonal fiction. *Peter's joy in experiencing the first snow of the winter.*

(1964) Sendak, Maurice. *Where the Wild Things Are,* illustrated by the author. New York: Harper & Row, 1963. 40 pages. Fantasy. *Max, in trouble with his mother, fantasizes a world of monsters where he is in charge.*

(1965) de Regniers, Beatrice Schenk. *May I Bring a Friend?,* illustrated by Beni Montresor. New York: Atheneum, 1964. 48 pages. Fantasy. *A small boy brings unusual friends to sup with the King and Queen each day for a week.*

(1966)   Alger, Leclaire (Sorche Nic Leodhas). *Always Room for One More,* illustrated by Nonny Hogrogian. New York: Holt, Rinehart & Winston, 1965. 32 pages. Folk tale. *A Scottish rhyme of the man with ten children who gives shelter to so many travelers that the house collapses.*

(1967)   Ness, Evaline. *Sam, Bangs and Moonshine,* illustrated by the author. New York: Holt, Rinehart & Winston, 1966. 44 pages. Fantasy. *Sam learns the difference between "real" and "moonshine" through an unfortunate experience.*

(1968)   Emberley, Barbara. *Drummer Hoff,* illustrated by Ed Emberley. Englewood Cliffs, New Jersey: Prentice-Hall, 1967. 32 pages. Nursery rhyme. *A folk rhyme about the building and firing of a cannon.*

(1969)   Ransome, Arthur. *The Fool of the World and the Flying Ship,* illustrated by Uri Shulevitz. New York: Farrar, Straus & Giroux, 1968. 48 pages. Folk tale. *A Russian folk tale of how the Fool of the World brought a flying ship to the czar and won the hand of the princess.*

(1970)   Steig, William. *Sylvester and the Magic Pebble,* illustrated by the author. New York: Windmill Books/Simon & Schuster, 1969. 32 pages. Fantasy. *Sylvester, a donkey, finds a pebble that he discovers is magic. Forgetting it is magic, in a moment of danger, he wishes himself a rock. He remains a rock until his parents release the magic.*

(1971)   Haley, Gail. *A Story, A Story: An African Tale,* illustrated by the author. New York: Atheneum, 1970. 36 pages. Folk tale. *A story explaining where all the African folk tales originated.*

(1972)   Hogrogian, Nonny. *One Fine Day,* illustrated by the author. New York: Macmillan, 1971. 32 pages. Folk tale. *An accumulative story of a fox who drinks an old woman's milk and gets his tail chopped off. To get it sewn back on, he must replace the milk.*

(1973)   Mosel, Arlene. *The Funny Little Woman,* illustrated by Blair Lent. New York: E. P. Dutton, 1972. 40 pages. Folk tale. *A little old Japanese woman has unusual experiences when she follows a runaway dumpling into a world beneath the earth.*

(1974)   Zemach, Harve. *Duffy and the Devil,* illustrated by Margot Zemach. New York: Farrar, Straus & Giroux, 1973. 40 pages. Folk tale. *An old English folk tale similar to* **Rumplestiltskin.**

(1975)   McDermott, Gerald. *Arrow to the Sun,* illustrated by the author. New York: Viking, 1974. 44 pages. Folk tale. *A Pueblo Indian tale of how a boy received the spark of life and had to prove himself worthy.*

(1976)   Aardema, Verna. *Why Mosquitoes Buzz in People's Ears,* illustrated by Leo and Diane Dillon. New York: Dial, 1975. 32 pages. Folk tale. *An African accumulative tale beginning with Mosquito telling Iguana a tall tale.*

(1977)   Musgrove, Margaret. *Ashanti to Zulu,* illustrated by Leo and Diane Dillon. New York: Dial, 1976. 32 pages. Alphabet book. *A unique expression of customs and ceremonies of African tribes from A to Z.*

(1978)   Spier, Peter. *Noah's Ark,* illustrated by the author. Garden City, New York: Doubleday, 1977. 48 pages. Religious nonfiction. *A wordless pictorial delight of the biblical story of Noah and the Great Flood.*

(1979) Goble, Paul. *The Girl Who Loved Wild Horses*, illustrated by the author. Scarsdale, New York: Bradbury, 1978. 32 pages. Fantasy. *The story of a Native American girl's love for horses and her people's belief that she joined the herd.*

(1980) Hall, Donald. *Ox-Cart Man*, illustrated by Barbara Cooney. New York: Viking, 1979. 40 pages. Historical fiction. *A year in the life of an early New England man and his family.*

(1981) Lobel, Arnold. *Fables*, illustrated by the author. New York: Harper & Row, 1980. 41 pages. Fantasy. *A collection of warm and amusing original fables.*

(1982) Van Allsburg, Chris. *Jumanji*, illustrated by the author. Boston: Houghton Mifflin, 1981. Fantasy. *Strange and extraordinary happenings that occur when Judy and Peter play a game they find in the park.*

(1983) Cendrars, Blaise. *Shadow*, translated and illustrated by Marcia Brown. New York: Charles Scribner's Sons, 1982. 32 pages. Poetry. *Marcia Brown's translation of Cendrars' Shadow, showing the enveloping, all-encompassing influence of the shadow in our life.*

(1984) Provensen, Alice and Martin. *The Glorious Flight*, illustrated by the authors. New York: Viking, 1983. 39 pages. Historical episode. *Louis Blèriot's experiments with early aviation leading to his successful flight across the English Channel in 1909.*

(1985) Hodges, Margaret. *Saint George and the Dragon*, illustrated by Trina Schart Hyman. Boston: Little, Brown, 1984. 32 pages. Legend. *A retelling of the story from Edmund Spenser's The Fairy Queen. The Red Cross Knight victoriously battles the dragon, winning the hand of Princess Una and earning the title of Saint George of Merry England.*

(1986) Van Allsburg, Chris. *The Polar Express*, illustrated by the author. Boston: Houghton Mifflin, 1985. 32 pages. *A small boy experiences a mysterious Christmas Eve train ride to the North Pole where he receives a silver bell that can be heard only by children.*

(1987) Yorinks, Arthur. *Hey, Al*, illustrated by Richard Egielski. New York: Fararr, Straus and Giroux, 1986. Unpaged. *Al and his dog Eddie, tired of the drudgery of life in the city, eagerly accept a mysterious bird's offer to be his guests at a beautiful island in the sky.*

(1988) Yolan, Jane. *Owl Moon.* Illustrated by John Schoenherr. New York: Philomel Books, 1987, Unpaged. Seasonal fiction. *Sometimes you see an owl, sometimes you don't. A small girl and her pa go owling on a crisp, clear winter night, hoping this will be a night when you do.*

(1989) Ackerman, Karen. *Song and Dance Man.* Illustrated by Stephen Gammell. New York: Alfred A. Knopf, 1988. Unpaged. Realistic fiction. *Grandpa no longer dances on the Vaudeville stage, but one day we spend a magical hour with his song and dance routine.*

(1990) Young, Ed. *Lon Po Po.* Illustrated by the author. New York: Philomel Books, 1989. Unpaged. Folk tale. *A Chinese version of the Little Red Riding Hood tale involving three young girls who outwit Granny Wolf.*

(1991) Macauley David. *Black and White*. Illustrated by the author. Boston: Houghton Mifflin Co., 1990. Unpaged. Conceptual. *Is it one story with four parts? Is it four stories? This book must not only be read, it must be explored. Each exploration will reward the reader with an unusual fresh perspective.*

(1992) Wiesner, David. *Tuesday*. Illustrated by the author. New York: Clarion Books, 1991. Unpaged. Fantasy. *The fantastic nocturnal event that began Tuesday evening, around eight.*

(1993) McCully, Emily Arnold. *Mirette on the High Wire*. Illustrated by the author. New York: G.P. Putnam's Sons, 1992. Unpaged. Historical fiction. *Mirette and the great Bellini change roles when Mirette, the student, restores the confidence to Bellini, the master.*